Map Your Life

Getting from Here to There

Lee Wilson

renownpublishing

Renown Publishing
www.renownpublishing.com

Map Your Life / Lee Wilson
ISBN-13: 978-1-952602-33-7

To my beautiful bride and queen, Tonya—the sugar in my Kool-Aid, my morning sunrise and evening sunset— and to my princesses, Alexis and Jordan. I am proud to be your dad.

I have made every effort to always put you first and to make sure every sacrifice was worth it. I cannot thank you enough for being in my life and supporting me by taking this journey with me. I love you all so much.

To my mother, Norma Jean.

I know you are cheering and bragging on me in Heaven. Thank you, Momma, for always believing in me and for being my number one fan! I love and miss you.

I'm thankful to my Lord and Savior, Jesus Christ.

You challenged a sixteen-year-old young man from the projects of Houston to regularly visit an airport where you showed him a dream. The dream became a calling, and that calling gives my life purpose every day.

Acknowledgments

To Renown Publishing: Thank you for the opportunity to publish the first of many books I hope to write. I'm grateful for your resources and your skilled team that has helped me turn my life lessons and experiences into a book that will make a difference in this generation.

To Brandi Ginty of Inkible: There is no one else I would rather have supporting me to fulfill this lifelong dream. Thanks for pushing forward and keeping me focused on the end game. Let's keep changing the world together. You make me better, Boss Lady!

To Mel Chapman: No matter the time constraints, no matter the crazy idea, you always creatively support leewilson.life with the best you have. Thank you!

To Addison and Tatiana Spears: The concept and design cover of this book was everything I could have hoped for. I could not do all I do without the creative genius of Team Spears.

To Tony and Dorothy Clarke: Thank you for all your support and prayers, and for always being my extended family.

To Nick Kennedy: Thank you for being my forever life coach. Your wisdom has changed my life.

To the Green Team, my UL Family: Thank you for believing in me and for pushing me to fulfill the vision in my heart.

To all the churches, pastors, and students who backed and supported my vision—especially Mark and Karla Hall, Kola and Lola Alao, Pastor Erik Lawson and Element Church, and my dear friend Richard Carver of Think Little: May God return your investment in my vision one-hundredfold. To Bishop I.V. and Dr. Bridget Hilliard: There are not enough words to express my gratitude and appreciation toward you. From the age of thirteen years old to this very moment, the life lessons you taught me are still being applied. You both helped mold me into the man, husband, father, and minister I am today. Bishop, you were my mentor before it became popular. I would not be who I am without you. I am forever grateful for your example and leadership in my life.

To Pastor Willie George and the Church on the Move community: Thank you for giving me a place where my gifts and talents could grow, and where my passion to reach the next generation was developed and gained momentum.

To Blaine Bartel: Man, we have walked alongside each other through the good and the bad, through the happy and the hard. I could not ask for a better friend or mentor. Thank you for being instrumental in giving the younger me an opportunity to fulfill my vision and for always reminding me of what I'm here to do. Love you, Bro.

To Pastor John and Lisa Carter and my Abundant Life church family: Thank you for pastoring me and my family, and for giving us a home in Syracuse where we could flourish and grow.

To my extended family—Shawn, Tamiko, Roscoe, Angeline, Paul, Kofi, Mike, Archie, and Melissa: Pursuing your vision and God-given purpose is never easy, and it would have been impossible for me to achieve without the love, friendship, encouragement, strength, and sacrifice you all have made over the years. No matter how seemingly insane or impossible the idea and vision I had, you were always ready to go for it. And we did. I am forever grateful and thankful for you.

And finally, to my family and foundation—Cedric, Tonya, Deborah, Chris, Byron, Brandon, Dillion, Nedra, JaNae, and George (aka, Dad), Anaiir, Jason, Jonas, Jaylen, Baritta, and Donis: Thank you for always trusting me and supporting me. Thank you for believing in me and loving me. Thank you for always being there and for being the support system I can always rely on. Family, first and always. Love you.

CONTENTS

You Are Here:
From Point A to Point B

I remember the first time I visited the Mall of America in Minneapolis, Minnesota. It is considered to be one of the largest malls in the world. This mall has its own post office and amusement park. It is big enough to fit seven Yankee Stadiums inside and comfortably hold thirty-two Boeing 747 airplanes. There are over 500 stores, with more than 11,000 employees working in those stores. It would take you days, maybe weeks, to visit all the stores in this mall.

I remember being in this amazing mall and not knowing which way to go. To navigate my way through the mall, I needed a very detailed map. Positioned conveniently throughout every mall or amusement park, maps or directories help us to identify where we are. They all have that "You are here" spot, and they give you an aerial view of how to get where you want to go. I knew if I wanted to get from *here* to *there* on the property, I would have to follow the directions on the map provided to get to my desired destination in this massive mall.

Getting from Here to There

We all have that place in life where we feel lost. Without clear directions for our lives, we can feel stuck. There's no momentum, and no matter how hard we try, we just can't seem to turn things around. Sometimes it's a physical place in our lives—a bad work environment or a toxic family life—but many times it's a state of mind. We so badly want contentment, fulfillment, progress, and success, yet here we are. Stuck.

If you're like me, you've probably spent hours daydreaming about getting from point A to point B. You've imagined life on the other side as pure happiness. The problem is that while most of us daydream about changing our lives, very few of us have the direction to turn fantasy into reality. We don't know what steps to take or even where to begin. We feel lost and confused, and we wonder how anyone could ever find their way out.

What's missing is the map that will take us from *here* to *there*. A map brings purpose. It brings intentionality. It brings clarity and hope and assurance. Without it, we wander aimlessly, but with it we can reach our ultimate purpose.

Your G.P.S.

If you've ever wondered if such a map exists, then you've picked up the right book. Within these pages is the *only* map you'll need to go from stuck to unstuck, from purposeless to purposeful, from a lackluster life to a life of meaning. It's designed to be that easy-to-follow guide you've always been looking for.

It all starts with a personal plan and strategy for results. In this book, you will have access to tools and tips that will help you to map out the details of your life. It's an application I like to call **G.P.S.** You have probably heard of GPS. It is a navigational app on your mobile device that helps you to know exactly where you are going, turn by turn. From one destination to the next, it shows you exactly where to go. This same concept can be applied to growing spiritually as well. I like to think of it this way:

[G]ROWTH—Stages by which a goal is first developed.

[P]ROCESS—Steps taken to achieve a goal.

[S]YSTEM—Set of activities working together to maintain the goal.

At the end of each chapter, you will stop to adjust your G.P.S. in a series of exercises designed to help you **g**row into, **p**rocess, and **s**ystemize God's map for life. The G.P.S. will act as a life map for you to identify and pinpoint those things in your life that require redirection, a tune-up, or transformation. Once you identify these things, you will take responsibility and steps of action. It's my hope that this simple activity will help you to take a new turn in life and find your way from *here* to *there*.

Now, don't be surprised if by the end of the book, you don't even recognize yourself anymore. That is exactly what I believe will happen. It's what I hope will happen.

On the road to getting unstuck, you will discover your greatest purpose. You will find gifts, talents, and the ability to do great things right where you're at, in this season of your life. You'll identify pivotal areas in life that are in need of growth and development, and you'll unlock the secrets of truth, decision-making, and taking action.

Ultimately, you'll discover how to work through every area of your life to make the most of your time here. The best part is that everything you need is already right in front of you: your Bible (your map for life) and a desire for change. You are the next generation. It's time to own it.

CHAPTER ONE

No Shortcuts Allowed: The Purpose of Purpose

The Bible tells us in Ecclesiastes 3:1, "For everything there is a season, a time for every activity under heaven." At face value, this sounds great. It means we can be assured that, at the right time, our purpose will be revealed to us. But knowing your purpose and understanding *why* it's your purpose are two totally different things. A purpose that isn't understood can't be acted upon.

For example, think of a glass. We can use a glass for many things. It could be a hat or a bowl for eating. It could be used as a step stool, too, if you were really motivated, but those things aren't its true purpose. A glass's true purpose is to hold things; this is its maximum potential. If we use a glass as a hat, it will likely fall and break. If we use it as a bowl, we will likely struggle to access the food we're trying to eat. If we use it as a step stool, it may hold us for a while, but eventually it will shatter.

As with the glass, you and I can do anything we want with our lives. But that does not mean that we are living up to our God-given purpose. You have to understand that the true value of who you are and why you exist comes from understanding the true purpose that God intended for you. Proverbs 19:21 says, "You can make many plans, but the LORD's purpose will prevail."

It is the Lord's plan for you that will hold up under pressure:

> "For I know the plans I have for you," says the LORD. "They are plans for good and not for disaster, to give you a future and a hope."
> —Jeremiah 29:11

The only true way to define the purpose of creation is to go to the creator. The creator is the only one you can rely on to understand your purpose, what you have been designed to do. You cannot simply choose your purpose. You must discover your purpose, and you can only discover your purpose by asking the one who made you. Only He can show you who you really are. After all, He has been preparing and planning for you for a long time (Ephesians 2:10).

You Are Not an Accident

You were always part of God's plan. Colossians 1:16 says, "For everything, absolutely everything, above and below, visible and invisible, rank after rank after rank of angels—everything got started in him and finds its purpose in him" (MSG). You are not an accident. You did not come about by chance. You are a part of this generation for a reason. You were made *on* purpose, *for* a purpose, *by* a God of purpose:

> *All praise to God, the Father of our Lord Jesus Christ, who has blessed us with every spiritual blessing in the heavenly realms because we are united with Christ. Even before he made the world, God loved us and chose us in Christ to be holy and without fault in his eyes. God decided in advance to adopt us into his own family by bringing us to himself through Jesus Christ. This is what he wanted to do, and it gave him great pleasure.*
>
> —*Ephesians 1:3–5*

These Bible verses show us that God doesn't make something just to make it. He didn't create you to meet His quota. Everything God creates is done with intentionality, including you.

Even the earth is so orchestrated by God that if it were any smaller or larger, the atmosphere we desperately need to support life would not exist. What about water? Water has no taste, and you can't smell it, yet no living creature can live without it. God made ecosystems and incredible beasts and beautiful flowers. Jesus said, "Look at the birds. They don't plant or harvest or store food in barns, for your heavenly Father feeds them. And aren't you far more valuable to him than they are?" (Matthew 6:26). If God made all creation with intentionality, then you'd better believe He made you with that same purposefulness.

God has brought you here for this moment in time. In the Bible, He told the prophet Jeremiah, "I knew you before I formed you in your mother's womb. Before you were born I set you apart and appointed you as my prophet to the nations" (Jeremiah 1:5). Your birth is evidence that God wanted you here and that you have a purpose. You are needed. More importantly, you are *wanted.* Let the weight of that sink in. God has a special plan for your life; there can be no doubt about it.

Once we realize that we have something we were made to do, everything changes. Life is no longer about doing whatever we want, or mimicking what we see culture doing. It's not about letting what other people think and what they say about us get to us. It's not about living in a certain house, driving a certain car, having certain friends, or stockpiling a bunch of money. Life isn't about chasing after the temporary things of this world. Those things will only leave you empty. It's not about looking to ourselves for the answers. It's about looking to God, the one who designed our purpose, for the answers.

Your purpose is so much bigger than your own abilities or intellect. Your purpose is needed so much more than your own selfish ambition or individual dreams. Your purpose is part of God's big picture for His plans.

When we take what's inside of us and add it to others' strengths and gifts, it creates greater potential for accomplishing God's purpose. All of God's children, working together, can impact everything for His glory. Conversely, when we try to run from our purpose, it messes things up for everyone. Consider a battery. By itself, a battery's purpose is to release energy. When a battery joins its purpose with a flashlight's purpose, it creates something that was not in existence before—light. One benefits from the other, and the result is something needed and more powerful than their individual purposes.

Our lives are much like this. When you freely add your purpose to the purposes of others in the church, they complement each other. Together, you impact the world, much like the battery and flashlight coming together.

It's one thing to be encouraged in knowing that God *planned* to create you, but it is another to know your purpose. The only way to get to know your purpose and your role in God's plan for the church and for culture—ultimately, your role in life—is to get to know your creator.

Your ability to impact others will only be as strong as your individual purpose to love and know God. This is our first and foremost purpose. You (yes, you) were made for a relationship with Him.

Knowing Jesus

God wants you to be close to Him. He created you to love Him. Living from this revelation and knowledge of purpose is the most important thing you can do with your life. According to Matthew 22:37–38, Jesus said, "'You must love the LORD your God with all your heart, all your soul, and all your mind.' This is the first and greatest commandment."

Our primary purpose is clear. *We need to love God, and one of the best ways to do that is through worship.* Despite popular belief, worship is not music. It's not singing. These things can be part of worship, but they are not essential to worshiping God. Worship happens with our lives and our hearts. When we go to the Lord in full understanding of how much we love Him and how much He loves us, when we feel emotional just thinking about our Savior, and when we reflect on the goodness of God and thank Him for all He has done, that is worship. Worship connects to God in a way that is powerful and intimate.

Another way to get to know God and be like Jesus is to love others. God has placed a purpose inside of every believer to love others. He did this because God is love. We are created in His image, so we *cannot help* but to love others! This is such a crucial part of understanding who God is that the topic of loving others is found in the New Testament at least fifty-eight times. When asked what the greatest commandment is, Jesus responded that the greatest commandment is to love (Mark 12:30–31).

For the whole law can be summed up in this one command: "Love your neighbor as yourself."
—Galatians 5:14

A third way to get to know God and, therefore, your own purpose is to live like Christ. This means taking on His values, His attitude, and His character. It means putting off our old ways and choosing to carve out of our lives the things that do not reflect who God is. It means being renewed and putting on right and holy living (Ephesians 4:22–24), choosing to live like the one who saved us.

To do this, we must let go of old things, old habits, and our old mentalities. The influence of your generation can be strong, but God desires to show a better way of living. We have to welcome change and seek a peaceful spirit. This means having patience with others, chasing after godly living as opposed to success, and being unwilling to settle for anything less than His best for our lives. It means praying through everything. It means giving our anxiety over to God. It means digging into our Bible, the place where we find all the promises of who we can be because of our relationship with God.

Finally, a fourth way to get to know God and step into our purpose is to believe our purpose is there, even if we can't see it or don't fully know what it is—

yet. Jesus is the greatest example of this. Jesus understood His personal purpose to do His Father's will and, from a young age, He spent His life pursuing it.

Pursuing God

There is a well-known story in the Bible that tells of when Mary and Joseph lost track of twelve-year-old Jesus. Can you imagine the panic? They lost the son of God, the promised Savior! I'm sure they were freaking out. I know I would be. They looked everywhere for days, and when they finally found Him, He was sitting in the temple, listening and speaking to philosophers and theologians.

Frustrated, his mother asked him, "Why have you done this to us? Your father and I have been frantic, searching for you everywhere" (Luke 2:48).

Jesus answered, "But why did you need to search? ... Didn't you know that I must be in my Father's house?" (Luke 2:49).

Jesus knew His purpose, and He chased after it with all He had. This is what it takes to experience your purpose fully. Step by step, moment by moment, we must choose our pursuit of purpose over the temptations of this world.

When I was seventeen years old, my pastor preached about a story from the Bible in which God told Abram to look at the stars in the sky and try to count them. When Abram looked, God told him that his descendants would be as numerous as the stars in the universe (Genesis 15:5). He told Abram to *see* all that He had promised to give him, and He told Abram to *believe* these things as if they were already in existence. Then God called him to pursue it.

This teaching changed my life. As I looked at the world with a future mindset, I began to see part of the purpose God had created for me. It wasn't the full picture of my purpose, but it was enough to challenge me to believe for more. It did not matter that I was living in the projects in Houston, that I had no father, or that I didn't know what I was going to do with my life. I believed God had a purpose for me. For years and years, I spoke to my purpose. People thought I was crazy. God had allowed me to see a glimpse of my future, and I was focused on pursuing that purpose for my life.

When I got married, I got to choose my groom's cake. I chose a globe with an airplane and the words: "Touching the world for the gospel." Again, people thought I was crazy. I hadn't done anything with my life up to that point that would indicate I would be serving overseas or touching the world. But I began to speak scriptures from the Bible over my situation, and I believed my life would change to mirror God's purpose for me.

Years later, I traveled to Africa, Asia, the Dominican Republic, and all over the United States, following my purpose for God. I believed God had a purpose for my life, and I chose to live like Jesus while waiting for it to come to pass. As He always does, God showed up in a big way in His own timing. But remember this: His timing matters more than our timing. Trying to achieve our purpose according to our own timing will always lead us to entertain shortcuts, and shortcuts never turn out the way we think they will.

No More Shortcuts

I remember the first time I got behind the wheel of a vehicle to take a road trip. I was driving a big fifteen-passenger church van on one of the busiest highways in the country—the I-45 in Houston, Texas. I must admit that I was extremely nervous and scared. It felt like I was flying an airplane without wings. It happened to be on a day when traffic was moving at the speed of NASCAR, which is actually very rare if you are familiar with the traffic in Houston.

Driving the church van on this busy highway had me very nervous, and I was sweating out of control. I was not sure if I could handle the pressure and stress of it, especially as I got closer to the downtown area, where traffic slowed down to a crawl and became bumper-to-bumper. On top of this, we had to navigate through the construction zones going on for miles. So I did what I thought would get me to my destination more quickly and easily. I took a shortcut.

I negotiated my way over to the exit ramp to follow the so-called shortcut I had in my mind. Let's just say that was a huge mistake. I very quickly found out that I was not the only one thinking about a shortcut. As a matter of fact, when I exited the highway to take a different route, it looked like all of Houston was driving in the same direction. Everyone was trying to take a shortcut.

To make matters worse, I got lost and all turned around trying to take that shortcut. What I thought was a shortcut became a major delay. I should have stayed on I-45 instead of changing course. Although it was slow and moving a little at a time, I would have made it to my destination more quickly than I did with my perceived shortcut.

So here is the big question: Why do we look to take shortcuts while pursuing God and doing what He has for us?

- We are looking for an easier way that requires less work on our part.

- We are looking to "save time," but in reality, we are being impatient.

- We are not willing to go through the pain of waiting, and we look for off-ramps out of God's process.

The reality is that we often take shortcuts not because we don't know how to get from where we are to where we want to be, but because *we don't like the price we have to pay to get there.*

If we are ever going to fulfill the purpose of God,

like Jesus did, we cannot take shortcuts. Shortcuts will derail your purpose. They present themselves as a blessing, but they are not the full promise of what God wants to do in your life.

When I played football, it was common knowledge that taking shortcuts during practice would hurt you on the field. Still, that didn't stop me from trying to cut corners. I remember coach walking past us as we did our drills. The moment his back was to me, the moment he wasn't looking, I'd ease up on my exercises. And I wasn't the only one doing this! Most of the team took shortcuts, making things easier when we should have been training hard.

When I got in the game, I quickly realized my mistake! I needed those training sessions to prepare me for what was to come. Instead, I was not equipped to play at my best. I was out of breath and missing big plays that I should have been doing with ease.

Shortcuts do that. They make it so we aren't fully prepared when it's time to step into our purpose. When taking shortcuts becomes a habit, we miss out. When we say "yes" to shortcuts, we are saying "no" to the big picture God has for us.

So do not throw away this confident trust in the Lord. Remember the great reward it brings you! Patient endurance is what you need now, so that you will continue to do God's will. Then you will receive all that

he has promised. "For in just a little while, the Coming One will come and not delay."
—Hebrews 10:35–37

God wants us to fulfill our purpose. He wants us to realize our role in our culture, in our generation, and in the church, and He wants us to step into the personal purpose of having a relationship with Him. Knowing and understanding these two functions of purpose are essential to being able to navigate the map of life. Without them, we have no compass. We have no sense of direction.

Step into your personal purpose, your purpose to love and follow God, today and begin the journey toward the great plan God has for your life.

WORKBOOK

Chapter One G.P.S. Exercises

G (Growth): *The only way to get to know your purpose and your role in God's plan for the church and for culture—ultimately, your role in life—is to get to know your creator.*

How well do you know your creator? Has there been a time in your life when you entered into a personal relationship with Him? When and how? How does that relationship affect your life on a daily basis? What do you want your relationship with God to look like? Write out a goal for how you would like to know God better.

_____

_____

_____

_____

_____

_____

_____

_____

_____

_____

_____

_____

_____

_____

_____

_____

_____

_____

_____

_____

P (Process): Four ways to grow in your relationship with God are worship, loving others, living like Christ, and believing in His purpose for you.

How will you be more intentional about worship, both in your personal life and with other believers?

_____

_____

_____

_____

_____

_____

What is a specific, tangible way you can show God's love to someone in your life or to a group of people He has placed on your heart?

_____

_____

_____

_____

_____

_____

Is there a change you need to make to live like Christ—a bad habit you need to let go, an attitude you need to change, or a relationship you need to reevaluate?

_____

_____

_____

_____

_____

_____

How can you demonstrate your faith that God has a specific purpose and plan for your life, even if you don't know what it is yet?

_____

_____

_____

_____

_____

_____

S (System): In what areas have you been trying to take shortcuts to God's plan and purpose for you? Are you ready to commit to His process and training, even if it takes longer and might be harder than you'd like?

_____

_____

_____

_____

_____

_____

Look at your goal for growth and the ways you listed to achieve that goal. What spiritual discipline (Bible reading, prayer, church participation, etc.) do you need to begin or faithfully recommit to doing?

_____

_____

_____

_____

_____

_____

_____

_____

_____

_____

_____

What ongoing act of kindness to others could you begin doing right now as an expression of love for Christ?

_____

_____

_____

_____

_____

_____

_____

Chapter One Notes

_____

_____

_____

_____

_____

_____

_____

_____

_____

_____

_____

_____

_____

_____

_____

_____

_____

_____

_____

_____

CHAPTER TWO

Are We There Yet?: Procrastinating Your Purpose

Have you ever struggled with procrastination? Several years ago, I promised myself that I would learn how to play the guitar. I felt like I had some worship songs in me and that the guitar would help. If I could play the guitar, I could express my experiences with God through music. I thought that it would make my time with Him deeper and more intimate, but things didn't go as planned.

I thought that the guitar would improve my time with God, but when I sat down and actually did it, I didn't feel anything special. I spent all my time trying to figure out this chord and that chord, so nothing really happened in my time with God.

So, I promised myself that I would take more lessons. I thought, "If only I practice more, learn more, become more skilled, then I will achieve the worship experience I desire." The only problem was that I procrastinated. I made excuse after excuse and never took those guitar lessons. Several years later, I still can't play the guitar.

I believe there are times in life when our intentions are pure and good, but our follow-through is terrible. The promises of God have been made clear to us, but if these promises aren't coming to pass in our lives, many times it's because we procrastinate when it comes to fulfilling our end of the deal. There is a part God plays, but there is also a part we have to play.

In the Bible, God's will for our lives is laid out. He has provided great and precious promises—over seven thousand promises, to be more specific—that we can claim in our lives as believers. Some of these include:

- "You have been faithful in handling this small amount, so now I will give you many more responsibilities." (Matthew 25:21)

- "I will give you back your health and heal your wounds." (Jeremiah 30:17)

- "Come to me ... and I will give you rest." (Matthew 11:28)

Why is it that we struggle with seeing these promises in our lives? I believe procrastination is part of the problem.

Putting Life on Hold

Procrastinate is defined as "to defer action, to hold off or delay intentionally until another day or another time."[1] The word first appeared in the English vocabulary in the sixteenth century. It comes from two words: *pro* and *crastinus*. *Pro* simply means "forward," while *crastinus* means "belonging to tomorrow."[2] I think of an old Spanish proverb that says, "Tomorrow is often the busiest day of the week." Isn't that how we tend to live?

We've so accepted procrastination as part of our culture that we even celebrate International Procrastination Week. It's celebrated every first and second week of March—depending on how long you procrastinate.[3] In the workplace, the average employee will waste two hours of time procrastinating and doing things they shouldn't be doing. That averages out to over 440 hours wasted every year while at work.[4] Think about how often you have procrastinated an important task, saving it to the very last minute, adding unnecessary stress to your life, and ultimately missing out in the process.

Consider this in a spiritual sense. How much are we missing out on because we procrastinate when it comes to the things of God? There are three ways our spiritual lives tend to be delayed.

Demonic delays come from Satan himself. The enemy comes in with voices and distractions, and he throws all kinds of things at us. The Bible says in

John 10:10 that he tries to bring destruction to us and hinder God's purpose in our lives. If we get trapped by the distractions he causes in our lives, we can experience painful delays.

Deliberate delays are self-imposed. They involve the things we usually ignore, things we want to do but know we shouldn't, or things we know we should do but don't. It can be good things, like going to church, getting rest, having family time, or doing work. We neglect them in favor of distractions or hobbies, like TV, movies, social media, or vacations. We can spend so much time doing things that don't benefit our lives and leave out the most important things that will help us to accomplish our purpose. In other words, we deliberately delay the important priorities in our lives and instead focus on things that aren't worth it.

Divine delays are from God. This is when He says to wait or to stop. It's when He says that the season isn't right or the timing is off. If you have been in a relationship with God for any length of time, you know about these divine delays that the Lord will bring up. They aren't procrastination, but rather an intentional waiting period for the right moment.

Our most important priorities should be serving, worshiping, reading the Bible, living in community with others, praying, and striving to change the world for God. All these things need to be in our lives, yet we tend to push them aside. The Bible is clear that procrastination is a sin. James 4:17 says, "Remember, it is sin to know what you ought to do and then not do it." How do we get so off track? Where do we go wrong? What leads us to prioritize playing on apps over reading the Bible and watching sports over making time to worship? I once asked on Facebook, "Why do we procrastinate?" Answers ranged from humorous ("I'll get back with you") to insightful ("because we can") to emotional ("selfishness"). Some people blamed things such as the Internet, social media, streaming services, YouTube, Google, and smart devices.

I believe all these things can cause some form of procrastination, but these are not the *reasons* we procrastinate. They can be distractions, just like anything else, but at some point, we *allow* the distraction to take over. Why do we do this? Why do we *allow* ourselves to be so distracted?

I believe there are four reasons we allow those distractions and procrastinate on our purpose.

Reason 1: Laziness

We are all guilty of being lazy when there are things we are supposed to do. It happens. But the hard truth is that miracles don't happen for lazy people. You will not see the blessings of God in your life if you are lazy in your walk with God, in your prayer life, in your worship, or in your responsibilities.

Mark 5:24–34 tells the story of the woman with the

issue of blood. She had been living with this illness for much of her life, but when she got word that Jesus was coming to town, she said, "I'm not going to be lazy. I'm going to do everything I can to bring God's promises to pass in my life." When He passed by, she dared to touch His robe.

This woman wasn't the only person there who needed Jesus' help, but something about her touching Jesus was different. Jesus understood the importance of the moment and responded immediately. "Who touched my robe?" He asked as the woman was healed (Mark 5:30).

This woman didn't sit back and wait for something to happen. She did not pass on the opportunity before her. She *did* something about her condition, and the power of God moved to heal her. She *made* something happen, pairing her faith with action, and Jesus understood the importance of what had happened.

I want you to understand the importance of it, too. You will not experience the fullness of God's purpose in your life if you are lazy. The Bible refers to laziness as a sin. The book of Proverbs speaks about laziness fourteen times, calling it slothfulness and being a sluggard. And here's a real awakening: laziness will not only lead to procrastination; laziness will lead you into poverty.

Proverbs 19:24 says, "Some people dig a fork into the pie but are too lazy to raise it to their mouth" (MSG). Think about your favorite pie. Now imagine it sitting right in front of you, but you can't taste it because you're too lazy to cut a piece and eat it. It sounds ridiculous. Who would be too lazy to eat pie? Yet this is exactly how we treat God's blessings. If we are lazy, we will never experience His blessings. God has so many pieces of the pie that He wants us to have, but many of us won't raise our hands to take hold of what He offers. We put off worship, reading the Bible, serving others, and more. All the while, God is sitting there with a pie of blessing, waiting to give it to us!

When I was a teenager, I was known for sleeping late—really late. I would sleep half the day away. Ironically, I also became frustrated when my life didn't look the way I wanted it to look. My pastor found out about my habits, and he challenged me. He asked, "Lee, are you a man of God?"

I said, "I am."

He said, "I want you to know something. Son, it's one o'clock in the afternoon, and you are in bed, sleeping. The milkman is up, the mailman is up, and God's man is still in bed, sleeping. You get up out of that bed and stop being so lazy." And the rest is history.

I realized that I was never going to accomplish what God wanted me to accomplish unless I put in some effort. From that point on, I have lived my life differently. I chose to take control of my life and pursue my God-given purpose.

Until you rise up and grab hold of the pie God offers, you will never be satisfied. Your life will be full of trouble and challenges. You will miss out on God's best.

Take a lesson from the ants, you lazybones. Learn from their ways and become wise! Though they have no prince or governor or ruler to make them work, they labor hard all summer, gathering food for the winter. But you, lazybones, how long will you sleep? When will you wake up?

—Proverbs 6:6–9

I made intentional changes in my life, and now I can see God's plans for me coming to pass. I rise early. I'm on time for everything. I make the most of every moment of every day. I'm responsible. I don't make excuses. I work hard. And God rewards me for this.

He will reward you, too, once you choose to move from laziness and comfort to hard work and determination. Laziness is a choice with negative consequences. If we want to see God's purpose and plans for our lives come to pass, we can't be lazy.

Reason 2: Doubt

Uncertainty—or what you could call doubt—can cause procrastination. There are times in life when we become so uncertain about things that we really shouldn't be uncertain about that it can cause us to talk ourselves out of doing the things we know we should be doing. We wait and wait for some kind of sign or answer. The Bible says in James 1:8, "Their loyalty is divided between God and the world, and they are unstable in everything they do." It's one thing not to know where we're going for dinner; it's another thing if we know that we should start tithing, but we allow doubt to keep us from acting. We might prepare our offering and even give ourselves a Sunday morning pep talk. Yet, when it comes down to it, we let the moment to give pass us by. Then regret sets in: "I should have followed through!" The longer we delay doing what we know we should do, the longer we will miss out on the promises God has for us in life.

Reason 3: Unrealistic Expectations

If you're waiting or hoping for things to line up and be perfect, then I guarantee that you're going to procrastinate. Perfection paralyzes us, causing us to delay doing the things we know we should be doing. This pursuit of the perfect time, perfect scenario, or perfect person will cause so many young people in your generation to miss out on God's best. Don't find yourself among them.

This is one of Satan's greatest tactics. How many times have you sat in church and thought, "I'm going to serve God by doing (fill in the blank). I'm going to give it all over to God and get it together"? Then the desire for perfectionism sets in: "I have such a long way to go. Maybe I'll give it all over to God after I've cleaned up a few other things in my life. And maybe I'll clean up those other things after I've started a daily prayer time. And maybe I'll start a daily prayer time after I've gotten my schedule under control...." The excuses can be unending.

I've got news for you! *You* will never get yourself to a place where you are "right" for God. *He* is the only one who can get you there! You can't change you; only God can do that. He is the one who takes our weaknesses and makes them perfect in His sight. The Bible says in 2 Corinthians 12:9–10:

> *Each time he said, "My grace is all you need. My power works best in weakness." So now I am glad to boast about my weaknesses, so that the power of Christ can work through me. That's why I take pleasure in my weaknesses, and in the insults, hardships, persecutions, and troubles that I suffer for Christ. For when I am weak, then I am strong.*

We must go to God and let Him make us into the people He wants us to be. We cannot do it ourselves.

Reason 4: Fear

There is a story of a woman who was driving home after she had just left the grocery store. All of a sudden, she heard what she thought was a gunshot. She pulled over, and she felt something at the back of her head. She thought she was dying.

People stopped to see if she needed help, asking, "Ma'am, what are you doing? Why did you stop on the busy road? Do you need help?"

She said, "I have been shot! I can feel my brains coming out the back of my head!"

The people looked at her and said, "Ma'am, what are you talking about?"

When she pulled back her hand, she saw bread dough. A pressurized can of biscuits had exploded in the back of her car. She had been so afraid, so paralyzed by fear, that she had been unable to move. Her fear mistook biscuits for brains. How silly!

So many young people are stuck in place because of fear. We assume that the worst is going to happen, so we tiptoe cautiously through life, avoiding anything that pushes against our comfort zone or reveals truth. Think of all that we are missing out on just because we're afraid to move forward!

There is a story that Michael Jackson didn't like to sleep. He was afraid that if he went to sleep, God would give his songs to someone else.[5] So he found ways to stay awake. He kept himself conscious and alert because he was afraid that he'd lose everything he had worked so hard to gain. Think about how desperate that sounds!

Fear is a powerful motivator. It will destroy your life by causing you to put off the things you should be doing. David gave us the solution to this kind of fear: "I prayed to the LORD, and he answered me. He freed me from all my fears" (Psalm 34:4).

There was a time when I was afraid to speak. I

could teach in front of a couple of people, but bigger groups intimidated me. When God started opening up doors, I knew that I needed to release this fear to Him. I said, "Lord, I will speak wherever You want me to speak."

Soon after, I was invited to be a speaker at a church. This was a big opportunity for me, but I knew that another, very famous pastor was going to be at the service. This man was an influential and skilled speaker. He was very popular, with a large following.

Fear crept back in. I didn't want to speak in front of this pastor. He intimidated me. I prayed about it, continuing to worry over it, and then suddenly I found out that he wasn't able to be at the service when I was scheduled to minister. "Great!" I thought.

The day arrived for me to teach, and as I walked to the podium to begin, guess who walked into the sanctuary and sat in the front row? You guessed it, the pastor I didn't want to come. I was so afraid that at first I could barely speak. Then the Lord comforted me: "Didn't I call you here? This is My plan for you. Don't be afraid."

I started teaching, doing what I knew God had called me to do. I stepped into what God had for me, and before I knew it, the pastor I was scared to minister in front of raised his hand from the front row and said, "Hallelujah!" in affirmation of what I was saying. (In case you're not familiar, that's the good feedback you want to hear!)

The Bible says, "Give your burdens to the LORD, and he will take care of you. He will not permit the godly to slip and fall" (Psalm 55:22). That's my challenge to you. God is going to take care of you, no matter what. Take refuge in His protection. As we read in Psalm 27:1, "The LORD is my light and my salvation—so why should I be afraid? The LORD is my fortress, protecting me from danger, so why should I tremble?"

The Simple Solution to Procrastination

There is a three-part process that will move us through procrastination and into action.

First, we must take responsibility. Benjamin Franklin said that "the man who is good at making an excuse, is seldom good at any thing else."[6] We have got to stop making excuses for our lack of action. No more passing the blame, no more putting it all off until tomorrow. We need to take responsibility today.

A final word: Be strong in the Lord and in his mighty power. Put on all of God's armor so that you will be able to stand firm against all strategies of the devil [enemy]. For we are not fighting against flesh-and-blood enemies, but against evil rulers and authorities of the unseen world, against mighty powers in this dark world, and against evil spirits in the heavenly places.
—Ephesians 6:10–12

It's time we suit up and do our part to win this war against procrastination.

Second, we must put our trust in God. Ephesians 3:20 says, "Now all glory to God, who is able, through his mighty power at work within us, to accomplish infinitely more than we might ask or think." God's power, God's peace, God's word, God's direction—it's all available to us. He can work in our lives and help us to conquer the things that hold us back.

Third, we must start today. It will be tempting to start this process when things are better or calmer, when you're richer or older, or when you feel stronger spiritually, but this will set you up for defeat. Start now because "time is running out. Wake up, for our salvation is nearer now than when we first believed" (Romans 13:11).

First Steps Forward

Martin Luther King Jr. said this about procrastination:[7]

> We are now faced with the fact, my friends, that tomorrow is today. We are confronted with the fierce urgency of now. In this unfolding conundrum of life and history, there is such a thing as being too late. Procrastination is still the thief of time. Life often leaves us standing bare, naked, and dejected with a lost opportunity. The tide in the affairs of men does not remain at flood—it ebbs. We may cry out desperately for time

to pause in her passage, but time is adamant to every plea and rushes on. Over the bleached bones and jumbled residues of numerous civilizations are written the pathetic words, "too late."

Don't let that be true of your life; don't wait until it's too late. Get right with God today. Be the man or woman you're supposed to be. Be the person God is calling you to be. Serve God the way He has placed it on your heart to serve. Live for Him. Worship Him. Use your talents for Him *today*. Today is the day. Now is the time. Let's stand on Hebrews 12:1–2, which says:

> *Therefore, since we are surrounded by such a huge crowd of witnesses to the life of faith, let us strip off every weight that slows us down, especially the sin that so easily trips us up. And let us run with endurance the race God has set before us. We do this by keeping our eyes on Jesus, the champion who initiates and perfects our faith. Because of the joy awaiting him, he endured the cross, disregarding its shame. Now he is seated in the place of honor beside God's throne.*

In Luke 9:62, Jesus told His followers, "No procrastination. No backward looks. You can't put God's kingdom off till tomorrow. Seize the day" (MSG).

What things in your life are you putting off? What is God calling you to do today? It's time to hear, and it's time to act. Let's run toward everything God has for us. When we take the first steps, we will start to move toward what God has planned for us—what He wants to give us and what He wants us to do. We can't afford to procrastinate in learning who we are in Him.

WORKBOOK

Chapter Two G.P.S. Exercises

G (Growth): What are some areas in your life where you have let procrastination keep you from seeing God's promises fulfilled? Which of these is the root cause behind your distraction and procrastination: laziness, doubt, unrealistic expectations, or fear? Write out a goal that reflects your desire to overcome this root cause and the resulting delays in seeing God's best worked out in your life.

_____

_____

_____

_____

_____

_____

_____

_____

_____

_____

_____

_____

_____

_____

_____

_____

_____

_____

_____

_____

P (Process): In each of the areas where you have allowed procrastination to run your life, how will you begin actively taking responsibility? Why can you trust the Lord to help, empower, and guide you? What will you do about it *today?*

_____

_____

_____

_____

_____

_____

_____

_____

_____

_____

_____

_____

_____

_____

_____

_____

_____

_____

_____

_____

_____

_____

S (System): Ask a Christian mentor or friend to keep you accountable to stop delaying and allowing distractions to keep you from God's promises. Share with this person the areas where procrastination has been an issue for you and the specific ways you plan to take action. Set up in what way and how often they will check in with you to encourage you in fulfilling your goal.

_____

_____

_____

_____

_____

_____

_____

_____

_____

_____

_____

_____

_____

_____

_____

_____

_____

_____

Chapter Two Notes

_____

_____

_____

_____

_____

_____

_____

_____

_____

_____

_____

_____

_____

_____

_____

_____

_____

_____

_____

_____

_____

CHAPTER THREE

Licensed to Drive: Mind Your Business

We have all, at one time, held in our hands one of the most powerful tools in the world: *a crayon*. This unique writing utensil encourages you to think outside the box. A kid with a crayon cannot be limited. They color inside and outside of the lines. They choose whichever color they want. They create and edit without limitations or boundaries. They can draw whatever they want, however they want. What they think in their head and heart comes out on the page.

That's what I love about kids of any generation. They think that anything is possible. You give them a stick, and they'll turn it into a toy. Kids have imaginary friends. They run restaurants and cook for stuffed animals. They run a treehouse school, and they're zoo caretakers on the side.

Pablo Picasso once said, "All children are artists. The problem is how to remain an artist once they grow up."[8] Isn't that so true? I believe we are fascinated with asking children what they want to be when they grow up because we're looking for ideas ourselves!

While children have no problem expressing their dreams and creativity, the older we get, the more we struggle. "Who are you?" becomes a question we hate answering because the truth is that we don't know.

For as he thinks in his heart, so is he.
—*Proverbs 23:7* (NKJV)

The answer is simple. We are what we think.

Thinking Outside the Box

Jesus is the master of helping people to think outside the box. He challenges us to think without limits and to understand the power of the mind, the power of thinking.

Jesus showed us a wonderful example of this in the book of John. In chapter 1, Jesus called Philip and Nathanael.

The next day Jesus decided to go to Galilee. He found Philip and said to him, "Come, follow me." Philip was from Bethsaida, Andrew and Peter's hometown.

Philip went to look for Nathanael and told him, "We have found the very person Moses and the prophets wrote about! His name is Jesus, the son of Joseph from Nazareth."

"Nazareth!" exclaimed Nathanael. "Can anything good come from Nazareth?"

"Come and see for yourself," Philip replied.

As they approached, Jesus said, "Now here is a genuine son of Israel—a man of complete integrity."

"How do you know about me?" Nathanael asked.

Jesus replied, "I could see you under the fig tree before Philip found you."

Then Nathanael exclaimed, "Rabbi, you are the Son of God—the King of Israel!"

Jesus asked him, "Do you believe this just because I told you I had seen you under the fig tree? You will see greater things than this." Then he said, "I tell you the truth, you will all see heaven open and the angels of God going up and down on the Son of Man, the one who is the stairway between heaven and earth."
                                              —John 1:43–51

Both Philip and Nathanael might have had some doubts about who Jesus really was, but they were open to having their minds changed. They recognized that they had a limited understanding of what was limitless, and Jesus rewarded their openness to seeing outside the box of their imperfect knowledge. He promised that they would see things beyond what they thought possible!

What are you thinking with your daily thoughts? Do you play it safe, or do you dream big, like a child with a crayon? Are you focused on the possibilities of heaven or the limitations of earth?

When we really look at people, we can see that there are five different types of thinkers.

Carnal Thinker: This person lives to fulfill their wants and desires with a selfish, sinful pattern to their thinking.

Closed Thinker: This person is closed off to any new thoughts. Their thoughts are trapped inside a closed and very limited box, and it is hard to get anything new inside.

Critical Thinker: This person is negative or judgmental about everything. Their thoughts always seem to go to the dark side first. They love to rain on your parade.

Confused Thinker: This person cannot think clearly; their thoughts are always out of order. They don't know what they really want, and they don't have definite opinions on anything.

Christlike Thinker: This person surrenders to God daily. They give all their thoughts over to Him.

Where do you fit? We can be saved, be filled with the power of the Holy Spirit, and memorize the Bible from Genesis to the maps in the back, but if we aren't being transformed in our minds and our thinking is toxic, we will never experience the abundant life the word of God promises to us, a life that is growing and moving forward every day.

> *The thief comes only to steal and kill and destroy; I have come that they may have life, and have it to the full.*
> —*John 10:10* (NIV)

The thief doesn't come to us physically. He comes to steal and destroy, and he starts in our minds, with our thoughts. Just like the enemy isn't playing games, Jesus did not come and die just so we could merely exist in this life. He came so that we could be transformed—body, soul, and *mind*.

Mind Matters

The mind is our command center for living this life. Proverbs 27:19 says, "As in water face reflects face, so a man's heart reveals the man" (NKJV). This verse is saying that the core of who we are is in our minds and in our thought life. It's important that we get our hearts right so we can see ourselves as we truly are, children of God.

Everything that happens in life is done on purpose. Things may not go the way we want them to go, but we have an active role in our decision-making. From marital affairs to how we treat others, our actions are the result of thought patterns that we allow to form over time.

It starts as a seed planted in our minds, perhaps

through a bad relationship or even a movie we watched. Then we process it, dwell on it, and open our minds to it. One day, the enemy presents an opportunity, and we walk right into it. We have to be more prepared for these kinds of warfare tactics.

Mind War

James 1:14–15 says, "We are tempted by our own desires that drag us off and trap us. Our desires make us sin, and when sin is finished with us, it leaves us dead" (CEV).

Think of your mind as a computer. The human brain is arguably the greatest, most powerful thing God ever made. It transmits and processes millions of messages per second. It is the hub of your entire body, from the colors and objects you see to your emotions, feelings, and muscle movements. It stores information, too.

Whatever controls your mind controls you. There is a battle going on, a battle for your mind. You have an enemy who is targeting the arena of your thought life, so you have to be better trained for the battle to possess your own mind.

The enemy attempts to influence our thinking, which affects our decision-making. But the Bible tells us to renew our minds, to think the way God thinks (Romans 12:2). This is how we defeat the enemy before he gains a foothold.

Most of us don't do this. Most of us feed ourselves with whatever pleasurable thing comes across our minds. Lust satisfies itself at the expense of others. When the feeling of lust comes, we don't do what the word of God says to do. Instead, we feed those thoughts of lust. When doubt comes in, we feed that thought and then begin to doubt everything.

Whatever we feed will grow in our minds and show fruit in our lives. This is why we must take authority over our minds and reject certain thoughts, such as phobias, panic attacks, fatigue, and anxiety. We must guard against what we take in, too, being aware of what we're watching, reading, and meditating on. We must be careful of gossip, whether our own or when someone else is gossiping about us, and we must guard against bad news, which causes fear. We must beware of negative situations at school or work, which cause worry.

The more we meditate and think on the lies of the enemy, the more these lies will affect our emotions, attitudes, and actions. We have to change the way we think. We have to be more focused on the promises of God.

Standing on the Promises

John 16:33 says, "These things I have spoken to you, that in Me you may have peace. In the world you will have tribulation; but be of good cheer, I have overcome the world" (NKJV).

Our thinking can't be focused on our circumstances. We have to be focused on God's promises. If Jesus promised that He has overcome the world, then we can rest assured that He is standing with us against the enemy's attempts to control our minds.

Claiming Authority

When we said "yes" to Jesus, we were given an authority we can use to take back control in our lives. This means that when the enemy comes to attack us, we have the authority to kick him out! God defines *authority* as delegated power over the enemy, and He has given us this authority over every area of our lives, including the areas where the enemy is trying to attack. We must own this authority, but the only way to do that is to get the word of God, the Bible, inside of us. We must renew our minds and remove anything that threatens this authority so that we can stand ready when our minds are attacked. If our minds go down, then our whole lives will follow.

God is the source of this authority. If we don't understand who is backing us, then we will never fully reign in life. When we release our authority into a situation, we release God to work in our lives. That's why we have to get the word of God on the inside of us and it has to come out of our mouths. We need to take authority when we speak the truth of the Bible.

Another important thing that happens when we release authority is that we are communicating to our enemy that we know our spiritual rights. We must declare, "You don't have any say-so in my life anymore! I'm letting you know my spiritual rights."

The next thing that happens when we release spiritual authority is that we release faith to do unseen things in our situation, working things out in our favor. We may not be able to see its release physically, but it is happening. We must begin to walk in that kind of authority.

We are Spirit-filled children of God. This is how we should think of ourselves. It reminds us who we are and how our thinking needs to be transformed.

You have to choose to think more about the promises He has made to you and claim your authority over the enemy and his schemes. This is how we can navigate the twists and turns of life that threaten to throw us off course. By taking control of our minds and claiming authority, we can beat any obstacle if we trust in God. And if we are beating the obstacles the enemy throws at us, it opens the doors for us to live the abundant life God promised to us.

Managing the Abundant Life

Living the abundant life is a choice of mind over matter. Think of it this way: if you don't mind, it won't matter. Your life will continue to be the same, day after day. You will be living by your own code of comfort, but you will never reach true fulfillment and abundance. We need to choose the attitude expressed in Psalm 119:112: "I am determined to keep your decrees to the very end."

We must choose *today* to obey God's word and live according to its wisdom and direction. When we live by the world's standards rather than by the word of God, we aren't letting God transform us into who He has called us to be. Transformation starts when we let God change the way we think. The enemy knows that if he can control our thoughts, he can control and dominate our lives.

Some people are stuck, lost, and unhappy inside, yet according to the world's standards, they are very successful. They have a great job, a great family, money to spend, and endless opportunities. But they are hopelessly stuck because of their thought life, because of their fear of losing all those things.

The enemy knows that he cannot force us to do anything, but if he can interrupt or influence our thinking, he can cause us to develop a mindset that is outside of the Bible. This leads to making decisions outside of God's will for us, decisions that move us away from our purpose. Second Corinthians 4:4 speaks to this:

> Satan, who is the god of this world, has blinded the minds of those who don't believe. They are unable to see the glorious light of the Good News. They don't understand this message about the glory of Christ, who is the exact likeness of God.

Take Responsibility

Only you can take control of your thoughts. Sure, the enemy might have taken up space in your life, but only you can choose to kick him out and take back what's yours. If you don't take responsibility for the way you think and how you direct your mind, you will never live fully in your purpose.

First Thessalonians 4:11–12 says, "Make it your goal to live a quiet life, minding your own business and working with your hands, just as we instructed you before. Then people who are not believers will respect the way you live, and you will not need to depend on others." It all starts with minding your own business, which includes being in control of your thoughts.

One thing you have to do to experience abundance is work hard to change your thinking. Just because you were saved and born again and you go to church doesn't mean that the way you were before you got saved has been erased. Your thinking was polluted and toxic. Getting saved doesn't change that! You have to detox your thinking.

The word *detox* is defined as a process in which one cleanses oneself from toxins and unclean things.[9] Detoxification is a natural part of the body. Your major organs, such as your liver, skin, and kidneys, process toxins to cleanse the body of waste and impurities. Our bodies go through this process to maintain good health.

Much like a physical detox, the Bible can provide much-needed mental and spiritual detoxification. Proverbs 4:20–22 says, "My child, pay attention to what I say. Listen carefully to my words. Don't lose sight of them. Let them penetrate deep into your heart, for they bring life to those who find them, and healing to their whole body."

If you're constantly living in past failures or past wrongdoings, you may need to detox from the past. You may need to detox from negative people, pain, phobias, a poverty mentality, or your own self-induced problems—whatever is preventing your heart and mind from aligning with God.

Proverbs 4:23–27 says, "Guard your heart above all else, for it determines the course of your life. Avoid all perverse talk; stay away from corrupt speech. Look straight ahead, and fix your eyes on what lies before you. Mark out a straight path for your feet; stay on the safe path. Don't get sidetracked; keep your feet from following evil."

We see two approaches to *guarding* in the Bible. The first comes from the word *natsar*, which means to watch or to observe with awareness.[10] The second comes from *mishmar*, and it means to guard with diligence, to stand armed and authorized to protect something against an enemy.[11]

To guard your heart and thoughts with *natsar* and *mishmar*, you must pay attention to what the word of God says and to your enemy's tactics. Don't fall asleep on the job! Tell the enemy to mind his own business, but don't ever let your guard down.

A few years ago, I got to go to Arlington National Cemetery. One of the most powerful things was watching our military go about their duties. I was especially impacted by the Tomb of the Unknown Soldier. This tomb has been guarded twenty-four hours a day, seven days a week since 1937.[12]

Before a soldier is accepted to be a guard in this position, he or she has to memorize seven pages of history on Arlington National Cemetery and recite it verbatim. Their duties remain uninterrupted during "heat waves, blizzards, hurricanes, rain, sleet, snow and hail." Soldiers take twenty-one steps one way, pause and face east for twenty-one seconds, turn to face north for twenty-one seconds, and then walk twenty-one steps back the other way and repeat the process. The soldier is not allowed to speak and will guard even during a hurricane (which actually happened in 2003).[13]

This is the perfect picture of *natsar* and *mishmar*. The preparation. The persistence. The protection. You must guard your life intentionally and diligently if you want to live in your purpose.

If the enemy can get leverage in your mind, he can impact your abundance. If you have a bad attitude, it's because you choose to. If you're not feeling connected to God, it's because you've chosen to think on things that are not focused on Him. We must guard our minds with intentionality. Second Corinthians 10:4–5 says:

> *We use God's mighty weapons, not worldly weapons, to knock down the strongholds of human reasoning and to destroy false arguments. We destroy every proud obstacle that keeps people from knowing God. We capture their rebellious thoughts and teach them to obey Christ.*

The abundant life is not going to fall into your lap. You have to do the work by detoxifying your thoughts, by taking off the old you and putting on the new you.

One Step Closer

Just like we obey law enforcement and do what they tell us, we must obey the Lord. The Bible is full of information on how to live and what rules to follow. You may not like rules, but rules are part of life. They are a part of growing up. You cannot mature if you cannot follow rules. If you want to grow in God, you have to learn what He says is okay and what is not okay.

When we do this, we are much better equipped to avoid the traps and tricks of our enemy. The word of God contains the laws of life. They are there to guide us, restrict us (in a good way), and protect us. They are there to ensure that we are empowered to follow the ultimate authority, Jesus Christ.

WORKBOOK

Chapter Three
G.P.S. Exercises

G (Growth): What are the thoughts, good or bad, that most define you and direct you? Which of the five types of thinkers—carnal, closed, critical (negative), confused, or Christlike—best describes your thought life? Identify what needs to change in your thought life and write out your goal for Christlike thinking.

_____

_____

_____

_____

_____

_____

_____

_____

_____

_____

_____

_____

_____

_____

_____

_____

_____

_____

P (Process): Become aware of what you are allowing into your mind and what thoughts you are entertaining. Where does the enemy try to tempt, frighten, or control you to influence your mind? Keep a bullet list for a few days to track the different types of thoughts you dwell on. Trace each back to its origin. What is tripping you up in your quest for Christlike thinking?

_____

_____

_____

_____

_____

_____

_____

_____

_____

_____

_____

_____

_____

_____

_____

_____

_____

_____

_____

_____

S (System): *We must own this authority, but the only way to do that is to get the word of God, the Bible, inside of us.* What are practical ways you can add more of the Bible to your daily life, such as a scripture memory plan or listening to audio recordings of the Bible? Begin implementing one or two of these ideas today. Ask God to reveal His promises to you and to help you detox from wrong thought patterns and replace them with true ones. A good place to start is memorizing Philippians 4:8 to use as a guide to evaluate all of your thoughts.

_____

_____

_____

_____

_____

_____

_____

_____

_____

_____

_____

_____

_____

_____

_____

_____

_____

_____

Chapter Three Notes

_____

_____

_____

_____

_____

_____

_____

_____

_____

_____

_____

_____

_____

_____

_____

_____

_____

_____

_____

_____

_____

_____

_____

CHAPTER FOUR

Guard Rails:
Reset Your Thinking

We all want to go to that next level. We want the next big moment, the next big break, the next big life event, whether it's a promotion, an opportunity, or a feeling of accomplishment. We hunger for this, and, unfortunately, it's often also how we approach God. We want to go to the next place God has for us—*right now*. Yes and amen! It's probably why you're reading this book. You want to move forward in life and in your faith, and that's why you picked up this map to help you navigate the way.

However, as we learned in the last chapter, we're not going to get anywhere without renewing our minds. Our thoughts determine the direction of our lives, so if we want that next place in God, then we need a new mind. And that takes time, patience, and diligence. It takes time to reset our thought patterns to reflect who God has called us to be—

people who represent Him.

In our culture today, brands are everywhere. For many of these brands, I could flash a logo and you'd instantly know the product. For most in your generation, you'd probably have very specific thoughts about whether you like or dislike the brand.

Over the years, God has shown me that we, His followers, are His greatest brand. It's important for us to begin to think about ourselves in this way. I'm not talking about being arrogant or living life as if we're better than others. I'm talking about understanding and appreciating the greatness inside of us. God uniquely wired us to be set apart from this world, to be courageous, to be loving. You have all that in you, and I have it in me.

We were made to reflect the awesomeness of God. As Genesis 1:26–28 says, we are made in God's image, the image of the Trinity (the Father, the Son, and the Holy Spirit). This is how we should think about ourselves. It's how we should carry ourselves. We are reflections of God! We are blessed!

It has nothing to do with being rich or wealthy. It has everything to do with being called for a purpose. God, the CEO of the kingdom of heaven, said, "I want to create a brand that will promote and communicate what My kingdom and I are all about. I'm going to create male and female human beings, and I'm going to craft them in My image. Then I'm going to live inside of them through My Spirit."

If you've ever wondered what your purpose is, that's it. You were born for a reason. You were born so that, at this specific moment in time, you could live out your purpose, fulfill your calling, and show the world who God is.

This is why what we think matters. How we think about ourselves matters. We represent the brand of the kingdom! That means we must not just walk but also think with purpose and intentionality.

I think of 1 Peter 2:9, which says, "You are a chosen people. You are royal priests, a holy nation, God's very own possession. As a result, you can show others the goodness of God, for he called you out of the darkness into his wonderful light."

Ephesians 4:17–22 explains the sharp contrast between God's brand and the world's brand:

With the Lord's authority I say this: Live no longer as the Gentiles do, for they are hopelessly confused. Their minds are full of darkness; they wander far from the life God gives because they have closed their minds and hardened their hearts against him. They have no sense of shame. They live for lustful pleasure and eagerly practice every kind of impurity.

But that isn't what you learned about Christ. Since you have heard about Jesus and have learned the truth that comes from him, throw off your old sinful nature and your former way of life....

Let that sink in. You are not who others say you are. You are not what your circumstances say you are or what past actions say you are. You are a new creation in God's image! But you will not benefit from your new position as a child of God until you renew your thinking and learn to see yourself the way God sees you—right now.

Changing Our Thoughts

Saying the sinner's prayer doesn't renew our minds. Simply going to church doesn't renew our minds. Being a Christian doesn't renew our minds. Yes, these things help, but they aren't the beginning and end of the process. We have to put in some effort. We have to work hard to rewire our *thinking* so that we see ourselves the way God sees us. This is what renews our minds.

What separates those who fulfill their purpose in life from those who don't is the way they think. Instead of waiting for circumstances to change, they change the way they think and move forward. Instead of accepting things the way they are, they make the changes necessary to move their lives forward in the right direction.

When we start to think better, we start to be better, and it begins when we pass all our thoughts and circumstances through the gate of the word of God. Just like when we go through security at a concert, we must bring every thought through the security of God's word. We must compare the things we're thinking with the truth of His word. If a thought doesn't check out, then we have to let go of it. For example:

- *"I'm not capable."* Well, Philippians 4:13

says that we "can do all things" (NKJV), so we've got to toss out that negative thought.

- **"I'm not forgiven."** First John 1:9 says that "if we confess our sins," then He will forgive us. If we've confessed, then we need to let go of that sin baggage.

- **"I don't have a purpose."** Jeremiah 29:11 proves that we *do* have a purpose because God has plans for us.

We must toss out every thought that doesn't line up with the Bible. Over time, God's word will build in our lives and act as a security gate that negative thoughts can't pass through. It will grow in our hearts until, one day, we have replaced all of the old lies with His truth.

Influenced or Influencer?

Renewing your mind should transform the way you make decisions. Romans 12:2 says, "Don't copy the behavior and customs of this world, but let God transform you into a new person by changing the way you think. Then you will learn to know God's will for you, which is good and pleasing and perfect."

To *renew* is to take off what is old and put on what is new.[14] We can't renew our minds by putting new things on top of old things. We must completely replace the old with the new.

This is why, no matter what is happening around us, our thinking needs to be aligned with the Bible. We all have ideas and thought processes that have shaped us. We use these to navigate life, to make decisions, and to think through situations. We may not even realize how much they affect our mindsets, but they're there. There are four things that shape these mindsets.

The environment that we grew up in has shaped our belief system. The things we experienced and were taught long ago shape the way we do life today.

The people closest to us have modeled a way of doing life that, whether we realize it or not, has influenced us. There are things going on in your life— patterns and mindsets—that point back to people closest to you and their influence over your mind and heart.

Constant media can greatly shape who we are. If we're spending hours every day watching the news, if we get sucked into an unhealthy relationship with reality TV, if we're consuming, consuming, consuming social media and not balancing it every day with the word of God, then our mindsets will shift to follow this information. The constant information we download—shows, music, movies, gossip, news—stays with us. Think about all that garbage you've downloaded in your life, stuff you don't even agree with or want. Cleaning this out is part of renewing your mindset. It's not going to go away on its own. We need to root it out.

And last, life experiences shape the way we think—our school experiences, our church experiences, our career experiences, the good and the bad things that happened to us. These things are still with us. They create the belief systems that we have today, and they may be poisoning our mindset when it comes to God and our purpose.

When you pool together all the things you have believed, all the things you have been exposed to, all the people you have known, and all that information you have heard over your life, then you will get the full picture of what is influencing you. All that stuff is the reason you think the way you do.

The Sanctified Mind

Our truest, most heartfelt thoughts reflect everything about who we are and who we are going to be. This is why it's imperative that we change our perspective from focusing on our own wants and failures to focusing on God—His love, His sufficiency, and His promises.

Here's what you need to know: God hasn't left us empty-handed in this! He provided a way to renew our minds and change our thoughts to be more and more like Jesus'. It's a process called sanctification, and we read about it in 1 Thessalonians 5:23: "Now may the God of peace make you holy in every way, and may your whole spirit and soul and body be kept blameless until our Lord Jesus Christ comes again."

Sanctification is a process, a day-by-day, step-by-step, moment-by-moment process of growth that lasts a lifetime. There are areas in my life I want to change, but God is still working on me. He is sanctifying me. Day by day, I get closer to a mindset that is molded after His as I do the work, together with the Holy Spirit, to change the way I think.

Don't get discouraged if everything isn't where it needs to be right away. God is still completing the job. He is still doing the work that He promised He would do, and it starts in our subconscious.

Our subconscious is where our before-Christ mindset, the mind of our old man, lives. It's where our old ways, our old belief systems, and our old values still reside. Our subconscious has been programmed to go back to those things, no matter how much we want to move on toward thinking according to our new man, the way God thinks. This is why we need to reprogram ourselves completely from the inside out. Until we change the way we think in our subconscious, we will automatically revert to our old ways of thinking when presented with challenges or temptations.

We need to drop the old mindset and replace it with the born-again-in-Christ mindset, the mind of our new man. We may struggle at first with wanting to revert to the old way of thinking (we always want what is reliable and comfortable!), but as we reprogram our minds with the truth of the Bible, day and night, our subconscious mind will develop new patterns of thinking. It will produce thoughts of right living, which will lead to a righteous outlook and righteous decisions.

Do the Work

The path to our new mindset covers three areas of change.

First, we must change our source of information. We need to look to the word of God as the new standard of living. As we dive into the Bible, we find passages like Ephesians 4:25–29 that train us how to live:

> *So stop telling lies. Let us tell our neighbors the truth, for we are all parts of the same body. And "don't sin by letting anger control you." Don't let the sun go down while you are still angry, for anger gives a foothold to the devil [enemy].*
>
> *If you are a thief, quit stealing. Instead, use your hands for good hard work, and then give generously to others in need. Don't use foul or abusive language. Let everything you say be good and helpful, so that your words will be an encouragement to those who hear them.*

The next area of change is with the people who are close to us. We need to surround ourselves with those who reflect the same desires and goals. As we have learned, the people around us carry influence, so we need to ensure that we are surrounding ourselves with good influences and good relationships that challenge us to be the best version of who God intended us to be. We can create our own culture.

Third, we need to change our environment, ensuring that we aren't putting ourselves in places that can easily sway us back into the old way of thinking. This means avoiding certain stores and communities.

All of this is essential to a renewed mind, but it will all be for nothing if we don't firmly establish the word of God as our foundation. That first step is crucial to success, but once you take that first step, you can begin to move forward to address a soul problem.

A Soul Problem

Your soul is made up of five components: mind, will, imagination, emotions, and intellect. Another way to look at it, in three parts, is your thinking, your feelings, and your imagination. The soul is the part of us that makes us unique. It's the place deep within that propels us to greatness. It causes us to laugh, cry, smile, fear, and dream. Our soul is how we love, give, care, and empathize. When we have a thought problem, we also have a soul problem!

We must renew our thoughts, our feelings, and

our imagination, replacing the old with the things of God. One way I do this is by blessing God. You might have heard it said, "Bless the Lord, oh my soul." I claim these words daily. I have learned to bless the Lord in my mind, my will, my imagination, my emotions, and my intelligence. It keeps God at the forefront of my life. Everything becomes centered on Him.

When we live this way, our lives will go against the rules of this world. It means being the head and not the tail. It means pushing out fear and striving for renewal. Our mindset affects our soul, and the sooner we detox our outlook on life, the sooner we will step into our purpose.

Total Renewal

The process of renewing your thinking is like tuning in to a radio station. Once you find the station, it's important to preset it so you don't change it. The signal may weaken at times—we are not perfect—but it can and will pick right back up the moment you step back in line with God and His word. The key to keeping in tune with God is to guard your thoughts and to preset the station of your mind to what God wants you to think on.

Philippians 4:8 says, "And now, dear brothers and sisters, one final thing. Fix your thoughts on what is true, and honorable, and right, and pure, and lovely, and admirable. Think about things that are excellent and worthy of praise." When we receive Jesus into our hearts, we don't just get a free pass to heaven. We get a new identity and a new authority. If your current preset is something negative, like jealousy, lust, guilt, anger, resentment, or fear, you need to reset it to God's preset. You need to recalibrate your mind to think about what is true, honorable, right, pure, lovely, and admirable.

One of the easiest ways I've found to gauge my thoughts is to give myself what I call a "Thought Test." It's based on Philippians 4:8. I ask myself questions based on the passage's challenge to think on:

- *Whatever is true.* Is what I'm thinking about honorable? Does it show the character of Christ?

- *Whatever is right.* Does it line up with God's standards? Is it right not only in my eyes, but in God's as well?

- *Whatever is pure.* Is it clean and holy?

- *Whatever is lovely.* Love gives; lust takes. Do my thoughts give or take? Do my thoughts encourage love?

- *Whatever is admirable.* Am I thinking about something that builds others up instead of tearing them down? Does it build me up or tear me down?

I challenge you to walk through these questions right now. How do your thoughts check out? Do you need to be renewed? Do you need to tune in to God's station? What thoughts do you need to take care of today?

If you can clear your thoughts and preset them to what is true, what is right, what is pure, what is lovely, what is admirable, then you will be well on your way to an abundant life, the life of purpose God has for you. God isn't going to force you to do this. He gives you free will. It's up to you to decide if you want to change. You must make the choice to live with the conviction expressed in Joshua 1:8 and dedicate yourself to the word of God.

As you begin to live out of your renewed pattern of thinking, the born-again-in-Christ mindset will eventually become your new preset, just like tuning to the right radio station and setting it to stay there. You'll be programmed to think and respond in a way that is in line with Jesus Christ.

Your new challenge will be to keep it that way. The enemy won't give up so easily. All your old mindsets and signals will continue to come at you. You'll have to stay rooted in the Bible to deflect them. You'll find yourself eager to get to church, to hear the next sermon, to grow in the Lord, to be around people who build you up, and to make decisions that honor God. You will be changed, and in that change, you will continue to have to defend your new thinking and keep it locked in place.

You will be the best example of the very best

brand on the face of the planet; you'll be an example of the kingdom. You will be choosing to live counter-culture for His glory. Yes, there are struggles. Yes, the world will call to you, but you will be more and more equipped to fend it off and stay true to the King's brand and the course that He has set for your life.

WORKBOOK

Chapter Four G.P.S. Exercises

G (Growth): How do you see yourself? From what, where, and whom do you draw your identity? How have your environment, the people closest to you, media, and your life experiences influenced your perception of yourself?

_____

_____

_____

_____

_____

_____

_____

_____

_____

_____

How does this perception compare to who God says you are and the new identity in Christ He has given you? Write a short statement about who you are in Christ and the brand you represent for Him. How does your thinking need to change to line up with this statement?

_____

_____

_____

_____

_____

_____

_____

_____

_____

_____

_____

P (Process): Look at the people who are closest to you. Are they influencing you to be who God wants you to be? Do you have relationships that need to be removed or redirected from prominence in your life?

_____

_____

_____

_____

_____

_____

_____

_____

_____

_____

_____

_____

Evaluate your environment, especially your expo-
sure to media. How are these things influencing your
thinking? Are there specific shows, sites, games,
places, or habits that are hindering you from living
as the person Christ says you are and has empowered you to be?

_____

_____

_____

_____

_____

_____

_____

_____

_____

_____

_____

_____

S (System): Are you committed to renewing your mind? Make a list of the "old" (thought patterns, habits, negative friends) that has kept you walking in your worldly identity. Next to each of these, write the "new" (God's promises, spiritual disciplines, church family) with which you will replace the old as you embrace your identity in Christ.

_____

_____

_____

_____

_____

_____

_____

_____

_____

_____

_____

_____

_____

_____

_____

_____

_____

_____

_____

_____

_____

_____

Chapter Four Notes

_____

_____

_____

_____

_____

_____

_____

_____

_____

_____

_____

_____

_____

_____

_____

_____

_____

_____

_____

_____

_____

_____

_____

CHAPTER FIVE

Turn by Turn:
The Power of Your Words

When we experience problems in life, it's easy to blame other people or the things that didn't work out. If only I'd gotten that job. If only that person would have kept their word. If only they hadn't messed up our relationship. This culture loves to cast blame.

Playing the blame game is easy, but what's difficult is looking at ourselves and taking responsibility for what has happened. Until we do this, we will remain stuck on our journey through life.

I'm not talking about being stuck in traffic or being stuck in a decision. I'm talking about being stuck financially. Being stuck in our careers. Being stuck in addiction. Stuck in the past. Stuck in a failing marriage. Stuck spiritually. Everyone wants to be unstuck, but how do we get there? What do we need to do?

A few years ago, I was speaking in Texas with a good friend of mine. He had just bought a Hummer, and he wanted to show me what it could do. He took me and two other people through the woods in the Hummer. He was just looking for stuff to run over when he spotted a huge mud pit.

My friend decided to gun it—and we got stuck! After three hours, a search party finally found us. They had to send an eighteen-wheeler tow truck to pull us out.

I remember thinking that it was a good visual illustration of how people are in life. My friend couldn't do a thing to get that Hummer out of the mud. It didn't matter how hard he spun those tires; there was no way he was going to free us on his own. Life is full of people who struggle with this same mentality. They have their own abilities, strengths, and gifts—they've been gifted with a Hummer, so to speak—yet all those gifts and all the money and all the things they have accomplished in life still can't get them unstuck when they experience problems.

There's a reason why this happens to us, and much of it has to do with the words we speak and the blame we place on others. When we look in the Bible, we see that there is no better example of this than the life of the apostle Peter.

The Power of Words

In Matthew 16:13–20, Jesus asked what people thought of Him. The disciples gave many answers, but it was Peter who said, "You are the Messiah, the Son of the living God" (Matthew 16:16). Peter was saying the right thing, and in that moment, he understood the power of his own words.

Jesus was so pleased by this that He began to speak the blessings of God over Peter's future (Matthew 16:17–19). Then Jesus talked about the crucifixion (verse 21). Peter, fresh off his top-of-the-class moment, boldly said that such an event would never happen (verse 22). He refused to accept that Jesus would die, and thinking of the moment that had just happened, a moment filled with praise, he spoke out of his false confidence. Jesus responded to Peter by saying, "Get behind Me, Satan! You are an offense to Me, for you are not mindful of the things of God, but the things of men" (Matthew 16:23 NKJV). Can you imagine how Peter must have felt hearing *those* words, especially after being praised just a moment before?

In Mark 14:27–31, Jesus talked about His death to come, and Peter swore that he would follow Jesus, even to the cross. But in Luke 22:54–62, we see that not only did Peter deny knowing Christ, he did it three times! He used his words to deny the very Savior he swore to follow.

How did this happen? How did Peter go from top of the class to the voice of the enemy? It's easy to look at Peter and judge him or be critical of him, but let's be real: we are no different.

If you have accepted Jesus as your Lord and Savior, He is with you always, whether you are at work, at home, at school, wherever. Even when you allow negative things to come out of your mouth, you are still with Jesus. Peter was just as much with Jesus when he was chastised as when he was celebrated. Jesus loved him the same. The difference was that at many points in his life, Peter's words were not reflecting who he really was on the inside and whom he followed.

By one estimate, the average person will speak 860,341,500 words in a lifetime.[15] But the question isn't how many words you are speaking. The question is not how elegant or smart your words are. The real question is what your words are producing in your life. Are your words producing life, or are they producing death? Are you reflecting God with your words, or are you reflecting the world?

Proverbs 18:21 says, "Death and life are in the power of the tongue, and those who love it will eat its fruit" (NKJV). I'm not denying that you may have some challenges in your life, but even so, it's important to make sure that your words *add* to your quality of life and don't *take away* from your quality of life!

Here's a story to show you what I mean. A monk is told that he can only speak two words every ten years. After the first ten years go by, he finally gets the opportunity to speak. The two words that come out of his mouth are: "Bed hard." Another ten years go by. On the last day, this same monk opens up his mouth, and what comes out? "Food bad." Another ten years go by. On the last day, he is asked, "What do you want to say?" and he says, "I quit." The guy over him says, "I'm not surprised. You have been negative the entire time you have been here." Words matter, and negativity adds up.

To get unstuck, we have to get control of our tongues. James 3:5–6 compares the tongue to a fire. A controlled fire is a good thing. It brings warmth and comfort. But a raging, uncontrolled fire destroys everything it touches. The tongue is no different. One word spoken out of control can set fire to your life. Words can create an explosion in our lives, positive or negative. That is why we have to choose our words carefully.

Words of God

Jesus said, "Brood of vipers! How can you, being evil, speak good things? For out of the abundance of the heart the mouth speaks" (Matthew 12:34 NKJV).

The words we speak will transmit faith or failure in our lives. Medical research describes speaking as the "most complex motor activity we do."[16] They describe this complexity in this way:

In the same way that a symphony relies upon all the players to coordinate their plucks, beats or blows to make music, speaking demands well-timed action of several various brain regions within the speech sensorimotor cortex.

When you speak, your body is reacting to the words you are speaking, good or bad. When we talk about being tired, we feel more tired. When we talk about being depressed, we feel more depressed. Our bodies have been trained to follow our words. I think of Matthew 12:37, which says, "For by your words you will be justified, and by your words you will be condemned" (NKJV).

In 1987, I was in Tulsa, Oklahoma, and about every other day, I was flip-flopping professionally and mentally about what I was going to do with my life. I was really struggling. I felt stuck in ministry, and I questioned God about my future.

One night, a friend came over to my house. He and I sat on the patio to talk. I remember being so frustrated with the way things were. An airplane flew above me, and I said, "I shouldn't be here right now. I should be on that airplane, going somewhere to preach."

My friend was stuck in his situation, too. He wanted to be a graphic designer and own his own company. He could sympathize with me. At that point, the reality of our frustration hit us. We were so pessimistic. We were wasting our words, wallowing in our self-pity.

That day, he and I decided to do something. We decided to hold each other accountable for our words. Even though things weren't going well at the time, we determined to encourage one another and speak good things over each other. When I would say something negative, he would correct me, and vice versa. This small change made a world of difference for both of us.

Are you truly thinking about what you say? I'm not talking about just speaking positively or having good thoughts. I'm talking about thinking on what the word of God says. Philippians 4:8 says, "Summing it all up, friends, I'd say you'll do best by filling your minds and meditating on things true, noble, reputable, authentic, compelling, gracious—the best, not the worst; the beautiful, not the ugly; things to praise, not things to curse" (MSG).

There are no other words in creation like the Bible, and here is why. Whenever we speak God's words, we are not just speaking good words. We are releasing the power of God to operate in its full power in our lives. The same power that split the Red Sea, the same power that raised Lazarus from the dead, the same power that raised Jesus from the dead—this is the kind of power that lives in the spoken word of God.

It isn't just a matter of speaking positively and speaking truth. Colossians 3:8 says, "But now is the time to get rid of anger, rage, malicious behavior, slander, and dirty language." Psalm 19:14 says, "May the words of my mouth and the meditation of my heart be pleasing to you, O LORD, my rock and my redeemer."

Speaking with the word of God means aligning our thoughts and words with His truth found in the Bible. This will not happen by accident. You have to be intentional about this. Every day you have to do a sound check—a spiritual sound check. You have to make sure that the Bible, the written word of God, is in your heart, in your mouth, and in your soul, because what comes out of you is only as good as what's inside of you.

Spiritual Sound Check

How do you sound check your words? How do you make sure that you don't get yourself stuck? How do you get yourself unstuck if you need to? These are great questions, but the answer to all of them comes down to what you really think and believe deep down.

It's easy for us to say, "I'm okay. God and I, we're good." But if we really search ourselves and are honest, what will we find? Ask yourself:

How do I really think?
What do I really believe?

You may do this and find that you aren't where the Bible says you should be—and that's okay. The biggest step is to acknowledge where you are because that's when you start to take responsibility for where you find yourself.

It's like cursing. People say that they curse accidentally, but there's no such thing. Cursing doesn't just happen out of nowhere. It happens because it's ingrained in the way that person thinks. It's become part of how they live and what they believe, so it comes out, whether they intend it to or not.

The first step is to acknowledge that deep down, you have a problem. Your thoughts aren't where they need to be; therefore, your words aren't where they need to be.

From there, you need to become aware of how God wants you to think and speak. You have to go looking for it. Don't make this something you'll change down the road. Take steps now to change how you speak.

Hebrews 4:12 says, "For the word of God is alive and powerful. It is sharper than the sharpest two-edged sword, cutting between soul and spirit, between joint and marrow. It exposes our innermost thoughts and desires." The word of God will get you out of bad situations and bring you into good ones, but you have to get into the Bible to benefit from it.

When I was growing up, my grandfather and grandmother used to watch the old black-and-white *Tarzan* movie. Sometimes Tarzan was trying to escape from someone, and you'd hear a scream and a cry for help. Then Tarzan would speak a word no one could understand, and suddenly animals would stop what they were doing and come from everywhere to help. That's what the word of God does. When we're stuck in a situation and don't know what to do, we can simply speak the power of the word of God, and Jesus will come to help!

True Transformation

The things we value and praise will become valuable and praiseworthy. The things we put into ourselves will radiate out of us. They will change our words and our thoughts.

Most of us think that we are stuck in life because of situations we cannot control. People say things like, "I don't have a job. If I had a job, things would be so much better." Or, "The color of my skin is holding me back. It's because I am this color or this race or born in this area or from this place." Or, "Everyone assumes because I'm young, I'm lazy and immature. So why try?" We attribute our struggles to things that are completely outside of our control, and many people are stuck in life as a result. But being stuck has more to do with what we're taking in than what is happening outside of us.

Are we reading the Bible? Are we doing a spiritual sound check? Are we relying on God to move us where He wants us to go? Only when we fill our lives and hearts with the word of God will we begin to see a change.

We don't have to remain stuck. We can choose to take responsibility to seek out God so we can move forward. Only He can get us unstuck and moving in the direction of our purpose.

Chapter Five G.P.S. Exercises

G (Growth): For a whole day, listen to yourself. Take notes if possible. Do you hear complaining, negativity, self-pity, or blame? Or do you hear praise, hope, gratitude, and blessing? Write out one way you desire to see your speech change to become more honoring to God.

_____

_____

_____

_____

_____

_____

_____

_____

_____

_____

_____

_____

_____

_____

_____

_____

_____

_____

_____

_____

P (Process): Evaluate your speech habits from the "Growth" step above. In what ways are your negative speech habits keeping you stuck and preventing you from experiencing God's best? Are there feelings or situations you are making worse by giving them power with your words? Review your goal. With what truths from God's word can you replace the damaging words you have been speaking?

_____

_____

_____

_____

_____

_____

_____

_____

_____

_____

_____

_____

_____

_____

_____

_____

_____

_____

_____

_____

_____

_____

_____

S (System): _The things we put into ourselves will ra-diate out of us._ Begin today to surround yourself with words that live up to Philippians 4:8. Besides regular Bible study and memorization, consider ways you can put God's words in places where you will see or hear them often. How can music play a role in shaping your attitudes and, thereby, your words? Who are some people who consistently share life-giving words with you and whom you can model your own speech after?

_____

_____

_____

_____

_____

_____

_____

_____

_____

_____

_____

_____

_____

_____

_____

_____

_____

_____

_____

Chapter Five Notes

_____

_____

_____

_____

_____

_____

_____

_____

_____

_____

_____

_____

_____

_____

_____

_____

_____

_____

_____

_____

_____

CHAPTER SIX

Under the Influence: Freedom from Toxic Relationships

The explosion of social networking is clear evidence that we live in a culture that is craving relationship. Websites and apps now connect people to talk, learn, and even date. The people of this generation are searching to connect, but here's what happens: a lot of the relationships we find on social media are not real relationships. Like figurines in a wax museum, they look real from a distance, but up close, they aren't really alive. The same is true of social media relationships. They don't require anything from you. They lack the intimacy, sacrifice, and care needed to form meaningful relationships.

It's in our DNA to be in relationship. After all, we were created in the image of God, and God is a relational God. In Genesis 1:26, when God said, "*Let us* make human beings in our image, to be like us" (emphasis mine), He was talking about Himself the Father, along with His Son and the Holy Spirit (also known as the Trinity). God understands the importance of relationship.

As believers, we need to get this part right because if we can't get our relationships right, then we won't get anything right in our lives. Everything flows out of relationship.

Relationship Types

There are a few things about the nature of relationships that we need to understand. The first thing we need to understand is that there are many different types of relationships, and they all come with perks and problems. Whenever you're analyzing your relationships, it's important to identify what *kind* of relationship you're dealing with.

Born relationships are ones we have no control over. We were born into a family, so we have relationships with those people—brothers, sisters, parents, aunts, uncles, cousins. A lot of toxicity can come from born relationships, and because of the nature of the relationship, it can be very hard to find a way through the trouble.

Business relationships are with people in life who can help us advance. They include co-workers, teachers, vendors, our network, and so on. These people can offer positive or negative relationships, depending on how and what they contribute to our lives.

Broken relationships are intimate relationships that have been shattered. Think best friends, exes, some family members. The pieces are there, but both parties are incapable of putting them back together.

Borrowed relationships are temporary and casual. They happen when we need people or they need us for a short amount of time. We may be physically borrowing from them (if we need money or help), or we may develop a situational relationship (if we're working together on a project). These relationships end as soon as the thread holding them together is no longer needed.

Building relationships are based on mentorship. They include coaches, teachers, and anyone else who helps us to grow. These people invest in who we are and help to guide us toward our potential and purpose.

Blessed relationships are based on unconditional love, with no strings attached. God is calling us to have this kind of relationship with Him and with others, but we must build these relationships from the ground up. They go far deeper than our average relationships, and they often require more from us in the long run.

Many people will come in and out of our lives while we are here on earth, and naturally we want to be social with them. But we must first understand the type of relationship. Once we understand the nature of a relationship, then we can understand how and why we should build it.

Identify Toxic Relationships

It is important to remember that God places relationships in your life for you to accomplish His purposes. I recently had an encounter with God while I was at a conference, and I wanted the experience to make truly lasting change in my life. When the conference began asking us about our relationships, it got me thinking. They asked, "Who are you doing life with?" God began to identify some people I needed to have in my life so I could be accountable to them. He reminded me that we aren't meant to live out our purpose alone.

There are examples of this all throughout the Bible. When Moses was chosen by God to lead the children of Israel, God gave him Aaron. When God spoke to Nehemiah to rebuild the wall, God gave him King Artaxerxes. When Jesus was sent to earth, God gave Him twelve men as disciples to partner with Him.

Just as God gave Moses, Nehemiah, and Jesus other people to help them, He also puts people in our lives. We can't succeed in life without these key relationships. They are critical to our future success.

However, toxic relationships will corrupt God's purpose for your life. The Bible tells us in 1 Corinthians 15:33, "Do not be deceived: 'Evil company corrupts good habits'" (NKJV). If you aren't succeeding, it may be because of toxic relationships in your life.

Relationships take place when two or more people are connected, associated, and linked with one another in a common bond. I have seen many people who don't understand God's way of doing things, so they begin to make up their own interpretation of His plan for doing life. They begin to create their own rules. And that's when it becomes toxic. That's when bad relationships grow.

Many of us don't realize that we're in a toxic relationship because we don't understand what toxic actually means. *Toxic* is defined as poisonous, deadly, harmful, dangerous, damaging, destructive, unpleasant, or nasty.[17] A toxic relationship is characterized by insecurity, self-centeredness, dominance, unhappiness, and unhealthiness. There is usually a repeated pattern of passive-aggressive behavior that can look like the silent treatment, subtle insults, and mood swings. You may feel like you are walking on eggshells and can't be honest. You may have anxiety and stress. Your life may even feel like a reality TV show with all its drama and high emotion.

Then there are those of us who know that we're in a toxic relationship but feel too stuck to do anything about it. Nobody likes to admit that they're choosing to maintain a relationship that is bad for them. Though it quickly becomes a point of shame, we feel trapped inside. We don't know how to get out, and asking for help seems like it would create more trouble than it's worth.

Toxic Marriages

We sometimes bring toxic dynamics into our marriages, and then we wonder why many marriages don't work. We expect our spouses to meet our needs, but the reality is that your spouse will never fulfill you. There is no one who can ever meet your needs like God can. Placing unrealistic expectations on another human being only opens the door to hurt, bitterness, and brokenness.

Relationships are like a tube of toothpaste. You get the most out of it when you're willing to start at the bottom of the tube. When we're willing to work on our foundation, our relationship with God, then everything will flow out of that. Nothing will be missed or lacking, and we won't look to have our needs met by people who cannot succeed in doing so. Only God can do this for us.

The basic building blocks of a solid marriage foundation are:

- Shared mutual interests
- Shared beliefs
- Established trust

- Selflessness
- Love
- Happiness

To have shared mutual interests, we need to have things we enjoy doing together. Having shared beliefs means having similar worldviews. To create established trust, we need to show one another that we can be relied upon, that we'll be there when things get tough. To achieve selflessness, we need to put the other person above our own interests and desires. We need to offer unconditional love to one another, even if we confront or argue with one another at times. We also need happiness, that feeling of compatibility and fun.

Our expectations can get in the way of these building blocks. Many times, our expectations are:

- Unrealistic
- Uncommunicated
- Unclear
- Unknown
- Unfulfilled

Our expectations become unrealistic when we entertain impractical or illogical assumptions about what marriage will be like. This usually stems from idealizing marriage as something that will fulfill us or make us feel complete. When our expectations are uncommunicated, our marriages can become distant or guarded. We are always looking for the other person to let us down. When our expectations are unclear, we only skim the surface of our expectations, leaving doubt or confusion. When they are unknown, we keep them secret and private, setting up our spouses and ourselves for failure. Our expectations will ultimately be unfulfilled and end up creating dissatisfaction and unhappiness in the marriage. In the end, unrealistic expectations will ruin unconditional love, trust, and intimacy. But God doesn't intend for it to be this way.

Taking Responsibility

So many people live in relationships like this, not just in marriages, but at work and with friends, too. At some point, we have to stop blaming the enemy, the way we grew up, our families, or past relationships and take responsibility for the state of our current relationships. Romans 14:10–12 says:

> So why do you condemn another believer? Why do you look down on another believer? Remember, we will all stand before the judgment seat of God. For the Scriptures say,
>
> "'As surely as I live,' says the LORD, 'every knee will bend to me, and every tongue will declare allegiance to God.'"
>
> Yes, each of us will give a personal account to God.

So many people are in dead relationships that were born out of unhealthy or toxic desires they once had. When you're on a journey, you have to pay attention to the directional signage around you. It's there for your safety. But when it comes to toxic relationships, it seems like we ignore all the signs, like the following:

△ *Danger: High Drama Area.* Some people are drama kings or queens. Even though we can see drama coming, we choose to stay. We choose to accept it as part of life.

△ *Warning: Very Insecure.* It's usually pretty clear when someone is insecure, yet we choose to stick around and feed their insecurity anyway.

△ *Beware: Lust Under Construction.* We know when our thoughts and motives are impure, yet we get into lustful relationships all the time! We violate our principles and our values.

△ *Caution: Ungodly Conditions.* Some people have habits that do not make God happy. Instead of doing something about it, we let it slide!

△ *Advisory: Unhealthy Expectations.* What causes unhealthy and often toxic relationships are selfish and self-centered expectations.

*Take firm hold of instruction, do not let go; keep her,
for she is your life.*

*Do not enter the path of the wicked, and do not walk
in the way of evil. Avoid it, do not travel on it; turn away
from it and pass on.*

—*Proverbs 4:13–15*

We need love, intimacy, time, companionship, affection, generosity, understanding, and compassion from others, so we bring all these expectations into our relationships. Meanwhile, other people are bringing the same expectations into our lives! The problem is that we're all trying to get from other people what we can only get from God. This cycle becomes more and more frustrating, more and more painful, and more and more harmful until, ultimately, it becomes toxic.

God's Way

We need to be upfront and honest about our expectations in any relationship, but we also need to recognize that only God can meet our needs. God's fulfillment of our expectations will always be more complete and rewarding than what any other relationship can offer us. I think of Jeremiah 17:5, in which God said, "Cursed are those who put their trust in mere humans, who rely on human strength and turn their hearts away from the LORD."

When you do relationship God's way, He will

meet the desires of your heart. You will have discernment, or an inward knowing, because you will be living your life open to the power of the Holy Spirit. The more you grow and mature in this inward knowing, the more you'll be in tune with the Lord's warning signs before you enter into toxic relationships.

The Lord will also teach you *how* to have a great relationship. He will show you how to deal with conflict. He will remind you about the importance of taking time to be alone with Him, the only place where you can find true fulfillment. It all starts with asking for wisdom and direction.

Ask God to highlight anything you personally need to deal with in your life. Instead of asking God, "Why can't You fix this other person?" or "Lord, let them see how awful they are! Let them see how they are hurting others," you will begin to ask God, "What is it that *I* need to change? What do *I* need to deal with? How do *I* need to grow? What in *my* life is not of You, Lord?"

This is where real growth begins. This is how you get to the root of something that's toxic because oftentimes we are contributing to the toxicity of a relationship just as much as the other person. Our relationship problems start with us. They start in the heart.

Psalm 34:17 and 2 Peter 1:2–4 tell us that a healthy relationship with God will produce healthy results, which include healthy relationships with others. An unhealthy relationship with God will produce unhealthy relationships with others. Only in a healthy relationship with Him can we clear out our lives of the toxic relationships that threaten to slow down our journey to discovering our true purpose.

WORKBOOK

Chapter Six G.P.S. Exercises

G (Growth): Evaluate the relationships in your life— born, business, broken, borrowed, building, and blessed. Are there any specific relationships that are toxic or heading toward becoming so? Write out your goal for each of these relationships, whether it is to step away from it as much as possible or to change your own attitudes and responses within the relationship.

_____

_____

_____

_____

_____

_____

_____

_____

_____

_____

_____

_____

_____

_____

_____

_____

_____

_____

_____

P (Process): Looking at those toxic or in-danger re-lationships, consider your expectations for each of them. Are your expectations realistic or unrealistic? Have you clearly stated your needs and desires, and if not, how and when will you do so? Are you looking to a human relationship to do for you what only a relationship with God can do? If so, how will you shift your focus back to God?

_____

_____

_____

_____

_____

_____

_____

_____

_____

_____

_____

_____

_____

_____

_____

_____

_____

_____

_____

_____

S (System): For the next week or more, pray about each of your toxic relationships. Ask God for wisdom about what role (if any) this person should have in your life. Ask Him to reveal to you your own wrongs that have contributed to the problems. Listen to His conviction and make specific changes in how you respond to the other person. Most of all, pray diligently for the other person to experience God and the abundant life that He offers them.

_____

_____

_____

_____

_____

_____

_____

_____

_____

_____

_____

_____

_____

_____

_____

_____

_____

_____

Chapter Six Notes

_____

_____

_____

_____

_____

_____

_____

_____

_____

_____

_____

_____

_____

_____

_____

_____

_____

_____

_____

_____

_____

_____

_____

CHAPTER SEVEN

Roadblocks in Life: I Love It, but I Hate It

There are things in our lives that we know we shouldn't keep around. We love how they make us feel, but we hate what they do to us. We may pray, believe in God, and have a healthy spiritual life, yet these things hold us back from fully experiencing God. They are the tripping places in our lives that we never fail to stumble over. Time and time again, they cause us to fall down. Even when we get back up and promise ourselves that we won't let them take us down again, we eventually find ourselves back on the floor because we never really remove the obstacle in our way.

Rather than getting rid of the problem, we hold back from full surrender. Why? Because even though we hate it, we love it, too.

I know it's sick, but we have all been there. I've been there. Paul said it best in Romans 7:15–16: "For what I am doing, I do not understand. For what

I will to do, that I do not practice; but what I hate, that I do. If, then, I do what I will not to do, I agree with the law that it is good" (NKJV).

This is no trick of the enemy. It's not even a trick of culture. We cling to these things because *we* have fallen into habits or problems in our lives that *we* don't know how to deal with. What are the love-hate things in your life? What are the things you don't want anyone ever to know about you, the things you hide from everyone else because they bring you shame, even as they bring you some form of twisted pleasure?

Those may be the things hindering you from the abundance God has for you, from the breakthrough and the victory He promised. They may be what is preventing you from moving forward in life. You may not even realize the pull they have on you, but you are intimately familiar with the love-hate relationship you have with them.

Sneaky Strongholds

Love is defined as "a deep affection or attachment to something."[18] We can feel love for many things, but as God changes our hearts, we may find that the things we once loved are things we are beginning to hate. This is supposed to happen. As you change to be more like your Savior, you will start to see the messy places of your life differently. Suddenly, they are not so pretty anymore. You start to see them for what they really are—tripping points.

Still, we feel attached. We've developed a relationship with these things, and it's hard to let them go.

Hate is defined as "intense dislike for or regret about something."[19] When things we love become things we still do even though we know we shouldn't, they become the things we hate.

This can happen if we're still going to clubs and bars even though Jesus has transformed us. It can happen if we're still looking at pornography, overeating, or abusing sex or alcohol. Anything you once viewed as fun, cute, and totally harmless can turn into something painful, regrettable, and shameful once the light of Jesus shines on it, yet it's still so hard to give it up. The old desires and habits of your life before Jesus try desperately to hold you back and keep you chained to the life you once lived. Even though Jesus set you free from that life, the tug of war inside of you between the old you and the new you doesn't feel free at all. It feels like an all-out war at times!

The enemy loves to play around with the things we love and hate, even as we keep flirting with them. We think, "I'm still saved, but that doesn't mean I need to be saved twenty-four hours a day." The world will try to convince you that you can take a break from being good all the time, but Ephesians 6:12 reminds us:

> *For we are not fighting against flesh-and-blood enemies, but against evil rulers and authorities of the*

unseen world, against mighty powers in this dark world, and against evil spirits in the heavenly places.

Second Corinthians 10:3–6 explains:

We are human, but we don't wage war as humans do. We use God's mighty weapons, not worldly weapons, to knock down the strongholds of human reasoning and to destroy false arguments. We destroy every proud obstacle that keeps people from knowing God. We capture their rebellious thoughts and teach them to obey Christ. And after you have become fully obedient, we will punish everyone who remains disobedient.

The enemy is waiting for a chance to get a foothold in our lives, and many times, these old habits—these things we hate but still do—offer him an open door into our lives. This is how he establishes strongholds, which are those habits or thoughts that hold us in bondage. They hide out in the invisible areas of our lives.

When I was growing up, we had roaches in our apartment. During the day, we never saw them, but at night, I remember turning on the light to get a drink of water, and there they'd be. We lived life knowing that they were there, lurking beneath the surface, camping out behind the walls. We just knew that eventually they would pop out at us.

Spiritual strongholds are the same. They hide out behind the walls of our souls, waiting for their moment to pop out at us. We rarely think about them.

We don't notice them right away. And then there they are. They speak to us in the form of doubt, unforgiveness, confusion, fear, suspicion, anger, guilt, eating disorders, worry, lust, shame, pride, and self-harm. Once these thoughts truly get ahold of us, they will create an outward manifestation of the stronghold within.

Strongholds convince us to give up and dismiss God. They can take control of our minds and turn us against God. They are the enemy's ultimate strategy.

Caught in a Trap

Satan comes to us in the same way he came to Adam and Eve. He comes with deception. He wants us to doubt God, so he fills our heads with lies. He deceives us into believing things that are not true.

Deception sets in when you start to believe what is false or fake. It is the root of being misled. First Corinthians 3:18–19 says, "Stop deceiving yourselves. If you think you are wise by this world's standards, you need to become a fool to be truly wise. For the wisdom of this world is foolishness to God. As the Scriptures say, 'He traps the wise in the snare of their own cleverness.'"

We are deceived when we hear the truth but don't accept it. We are deceived when we believe we don't have a sin problem. We are deceived when we think that there are no consequences to our sin. We are deceived when we think that we can live for God and the world at the same time. We are deceived when we think that there is no enemy or that the enemy isn't going to waste his time on us.

Satan is the enemy of anyone who chooses to live for God. His job is to trick us any way he can, and he lies about what will give us peace and fulfill us. His ultimate goal is to lure us into a trap that will lead to our downfall.

We know that we've fallen into a trap when our behavior reflects the world and not the character of God found in the Bible. We start to lie and manipulate. We isolate ourselves from those trying to help us. We willingly do things that hurt our relationship with God. Sound familiar? We hate it, yet we can't seem to stop. But there is a way out.

Our Only Way Out

We will never find peace and fulfillment through the things of this world. The world and all of its temptations can be defined as:

[W]ICKED—It is evil and morally wrong.

[O]PPRESSIVE—It weighs heavily on us.

[R]EBELLIOUS—It refuses to obey and kicks against authority.

[L]USTFUL—It desires the things of the flesh.

[D]EATH-PRODUCING—It brings about destruction.

The world is full of sin, and sin goes against God's word.

> You can't pick and choose in these things, specializing in keeping one or two things in God's law and ignoring others. The same God who said, "Don't commit adultery," also said, "Don't murder." If you don't commit adultery but go ahead and murder, do you think your non-adultery will cancel out your murder? No, you're a murderer, period.
> —James 2:10–11 (MSG)

The good things we do cannot justify the bad. When it comes to sin, we are all at fault. We all have things we do that we hate, sins that we choose to continue. We even have sins that we don't realize are there! The weight of this reality can be too much to bear.

That's why God sent Jesus. Because of Jesus, we can repent of our sins and be forgiven every single time.

> God saved you by his grace when you believed. And you can't take credit for this; it is a gift from God. Salvation is not a reward for the good things we have done, so none of us can boast about it.
> —Ephesians 2:8–9

I think about the TV show, Survivor. Each week, competitors try to win a challenge. If they win, they get immunity and are saved from being voted off the show. Jesus is our immunity. He died on the cross to save us from the very sins we are struggling with today. He died to take care of temptations before we were even tempted. He died so that we could have immunity *forever.*

Because of this, we don't have to feel guilty. We don't have to live under condemnation. While it's true that we can't escape the trap of this world on our own, Jesus can get us out. He died on the cross to set us free. Only He can permanently remove the hold that the things we hate have on us.

Free at Last

Many people in your generation will live their entire lives stuck in their struggle with sin. They beat themselves up over and over again, blaming themselves for their failures. They long for a way out, but they're trapped by the things in their lives that they love and hate.

Through Christ Jesus, we can deal with our sin. We can confess to the Lord and work through it.

> *So now there is no condemnation for those who belong to Christ Jesus. And because you belong to him, the power of the life-giving Spirit has freed you from the power of sin that leads to death.*
> —*Romans 8:1–2*

What in your life has become a trap or an addiction? What is something you can't seem to let go of? It's time to take it to the Lord. It's time to confess and receive forgiveness. It's time to work on that dark side of your heart, allowing God to shine His light there. It's time to pray and ask God for a breakthrough.

> *Don't be misled—you cannot mock the justice of God. You will always harvest what you plant. Those who live only to satisfy their own sinful nature will harvest decay and death from that sinful nature. But those who live to please the Spirit will harvest everlasting life from the Spirit. So let's not get tired of doing what is good. At just the right time we will reap a harvest of blessing if we don't give up.*
> *—Galatians 6:7–9*

Breakthroughs are a process. Just as it takes time to plant and reap a harvest, it takes time to experience a breakthrough. The Bible tells us not to grow weary or tired while waiting for a breakthrough, but to remain faithful. It tells us to keep doing the good things, to stay with it, to keep at it.

I challenge you to root out those things you do that you hate. Confess them. Work through them. And trust that God will begin to give you freedom from the traps in your life so you can live out your purpose, no strings attached.

Chapter Seven
G.P.S. Exercises

G (Growth): What are the things in your life that you secretly both love and hate? How have they kept you trapped or hindered you from living out your full purpose for God? What is your goal for seeing these sins removed from your life? Are you ready to remove them, or do you first need God to remove your affection for them?

_____

_____

_____

_____

_____

_____

_____

_____

_____

_____

_____

_____

_____

_____

_____

_____

_____

_____

_____

P (Process): What is the lie that you have accepted behind each stronghold in your life? What other sins have you engaged in or poor choices have you made to try to protect these secret sins? Ask God to help you see these tripping points in your life through the lens of His truth and to remove your love for the things you hate.

_____

_____

_____

_____

_____

_____

_____

_____

_____

_____

_____

_____

_____

_____

_____

_____

_____

_____

_____

S (System): Confess your sins to the Lord. Repent and ask for His help in seeing a breakthrough. Then ask a mature Christian friend or mentor for help in keeping you accountable to do the hard work of tearing down that stronghold and replacing it with the truth and power of God.

Chapter Seven Notes

CHAPTER EIGHT

Get Upgraded: Level Up

There are some interesting parallels between our lives and video games. There are enemies you're trying to defeat and obstacles you're trying to overcome. Your first run through, you're just trying to do your best, knowing that you will probably fail to get it right. But the more experience you gain, the more you practice, the better you get at preparing for those failures and roadblocks. You learn how to overcome them as time goes on. No matter what level you achieve, there are always more challenges waiting behind the next corner. There is always the opportunity to level up!

In real life, we are all trying to level up and get to that next level, whether it be in a job or a relationship. We need this same mindset when it comes to our relationship with God.

In 1 Corinthians 3:1–3, the Bible says that like

newborn babies crave milk, we need the basics because we aren't yet ready to take in more complex
spiritual food. We need Christianity to be simple and
easy to understand. But as we grow into the more
mature relationship with Jesus that He promised us
when He saved us, our tastes change. We want
more of God. We want to know more, learn more,
and understand more. We realize that no matter how
wise we are or how blessed we are or how much
love for the Lord is in our hearts, there is always another fuller, deeper level God wants to go to in our
lives. In essence, we will always desire to level up.

Made to Crave

When I first began to change and to understand
God's purpose for my life, I was bold and passion-
ate about my faith. I wanted to dive in deep, but God
told me that I needed to pace myself. I needed to
grow into my faith.

I told everyone I knew about the Lord, even
though there were areas of my faith that I hadn't fully
experienced yet for myself. One of those areas was
speaking in tongues. Speaking in tongues means
speaking in a heavenly language. Because it is a
language that is given to you as a free gift when you
are filled with the Holy Spirit and it can sound foreign
(even to your own ears at times!), it sounds like you
are speaking in other tongues. Speaking in tongues
can happen when you partner with the Holy Spirit

while praying. One minute you are praying in English, and the next your heavenly language can take over.

First Corinthians 14:2 says, "For if you have the ability to speak in tongues, you will be talking only to God, since people won't be able to understand you. You will be speaking by the power of the Spirit, but it will all be mysterious." It later goes on to say, "For if I pray in tongues, my spirit is praying, but I don't understand what I am saying. Well then, what shall I do? I will pray in the spirit, and I will also pray in words I understand. I will sing in the spirit, and I will also sing in words I understand" (1 Corinthians 14:14–15).

Praying in tongues is a gift from God, one that comes as a sign of your relationship with Him. When you don't know what to pray, pray in tongues. You will be praying by the leading and the power of the Holy Spirit if you do. All you have to do is ask to receive this free gift.

I remember being with a close friend at 1:30 in the morning. Right there on the basketball court in the middle of our apartment complex, he was filled with the Holy Spirit. He began speaking in tongues right then and there. I went back home and went into my bedroom. I got on my knees and prayed to God, "I thank You for filling my friend with the Holy Spirit, but I'm really believing that I will have the evidence of speaking in tongues, too." I wanted it so badly.

I kept trusting and being faithful. I kept studying the Bible. I received more and more understanding, and then suddenly my prayer life and my prayer language began to change. The very first time I prayed in tongues was a surreal experience. It was so impactful that I told everyone I knew about it. I wanted them to feel the same joy and excitement I was feeling.

Like newborn babies crave milk, we must crave what God has for us (1 Peter 2:2–3). We must seek it out earnestly and with hearts open to Him and His timing. The more we seek Him, the more we'll level up when it comes to knowing and understanding His ways, but it is an ongoing process.

No Quick Fix

Oftentimes we want a one-and-done experience, but there is more to serving and loving God than just getting saved. Yes, we are grateful for a change of heart, but there is more to Christianity than simply saying, "Jesus, forgive me" and "Jesus, I love You."

God has challenged us to level up in our relationship with Him, just as we are to level up in every area of our lives. We have to seek a stronger identity in Him, stronger influence, a better attitude, better thinking and speaking, and decision-making that's in line with Him. Second Timothy 3:14 says that we are to "*continue* in the things" we've learned (NKJV, emphasis mine). In other words, we're always the students, and God is always the teacher. There is always something new to learn.

God wants to be the most important part of our

lives. He wants to lead us every day of the week, not just on Sunday. If we want to walk in this abundant life God has promised us, then we need to give Him access 24/7—not just when we're desperate or in crisis, but also when we're happy and life is good.

The Bible confirms in 1 Corinthians 13:11, "When I was a child, I spoke and thought and reasoned as a child. But when I grew up, I put away childish things." It's time to put away childish things. This doesn't mean that you can't have fun! But at the same time, we need to get serious about the stuff God says is serious. As the Bible tells us in Matthew 7:24–27, we have to build a foundation so that when the winds begin to blow and the storms begin to come, we will remain steadfast and continue leveling up. With each challenge in life, we will experience more and more of Him instead of being blown back and forth with nothing to hold on to for support.

Leveling up takes intentionality. It's not a matter of looking up to the sky and asking God for a boost. It's not a coincidence or luck. In real life, there are no mushrooms that help us to grow up. Growing takes commitment and determination. The Bible says in 1 Corinthians 9:24–26:

Don't you realize that in a race everyone runs, but only one person gets the prize? So run to win! All athletes are disciplined in their training. They do it to win a prize that will fade away, but we do it for an eternal prize. So I run with purpose in every step.

With every step in your day, run like you're aiming to win the prize!

Skewed Focus

Too many things in our lives control us: our jobs, our worldly goals, our hobbies, and our relationships. Many times, we aren't leveling up because we have a lack of balance. We focus too much on the things that don't matter and not enough on the things that do.

We tend to blame culture or technology. We blame all the distractions, but the core issue is that we lack balance in our everyday choices. So much is coming at us—and it's not all bad. There's church, family, errands to run, exercise, work, and so many other obligations. We feel stretched thin, like we're being pulled on all sides. But we look around and see that everyone else is just as busy, just as overwhelmed, just as tired as we are. We think it's normal even though all the warning signs are there.

A sign that we're unbalanced is if we still think about work when we're at home or home when we're at work. We're out of balance if we're always fifteen minutes late, if we just can't wake up on time, if we can't plan our day to be out the door and on a schedule. We're out of balance if we're always leaving a calendar appointment early. Lunch with a friend? We have to cut it short by fifteen minutes because we scheduled something else right behind lunch. Son's basketball game? We have to leave at the start of the fourth quarter because we have to prep for a morning meeting. There doesn't seem to be enough time. When we aren't fully present in every aspect of our lives, then we know that we're out of balance.

The Bible hinted at this. Ecclesiastes 3:1–6 says:

> *For everything there is a season, a time for every activity under heaven. A time to be born and a time to die. A time to plant and a time to harvest. A time to kill and a time to heal. A time to tear down and a time to build up. A time to cry and a time to laugh. A time to grieve and a time to dance. A time to scatter stones and a time to gather stones. A time to embrace and a time to turn away. A time to search and a time to quit searching. A time to keep and a time to throw away.*

Consider this an encouragement to be present in the moment and not to let our lives fall out of balance.

Intentional Balance

Despite the Bible's call for us to embrace focus and balance in each season of life, for some reason, many of us can't seem to make this work in real life. This is a mental, physical, and spiritual tug of war for us. How do we bring balance to all this? Romans 12:1 says, "And so, dear brothers and sisters, I plead with you to give your bodies to God because of all he has done for you. Let them be a living and holy sacrifice—the kind he will find acceptable. This is truly the way to worship him."

The Bible wants us to lay it all down, to hand it over to God. Unless we are intentional and purposeful about creating healthy balance in our lives, we will continue to remain spiritual beginners, stuck at level one.

In a true and knowing relationship with God, when you find a natural balance, life moves at a different pace. I've found that the more I can control what's around me, the better I can think straight and prioritize appropriately.

Keep in mind that *living a balanced life is a matter of choice, not culture.* Proverbs 3:1–2 says, "My child, never forget the things I have taught you. Store my commands in your heart. If you do this, you will live many years, and your life will be satisfying." Proverbs 3:5–6 adds, "Trust in the LORD with all your heart; do not depend on your own understanding. Seek his will in all you do, and he will show you which path to take." This means that in school, life, marriage, career, finances, and everything else that we do, we are to seek His will. In return, He will show us which path to take.

None of us is perfect, and none of us will ever be perfect, but God wants us to live our best lives here on earth, and that means having balance. A balanced life means that we have an even distribution of time and priorities in every area of our lives. We know when to say "yes" and when to say "no." We allow everything to stay in order. God wants us to have this kind of balance in our lives.

God Himself demonstrated this kind of balance and order when He rested on the Sabbath. The Bible says in Exodus 20:9–10, "You have six days each week for your ordinary work, but the seventh day is a Sabbath day of rest dedicated to the LORD your God. On that day no one in your household may do any work." These verses remind us that we need boundaries to help us maintain our balance.

A Practical Approach

The system of balance that I practice in my life is what I call the LRW. It's an easy system for me to remember because those are also my initials! For me, LRW means that I choose to be intentional regarding Life, Rest, and Work.

Life. We have to be intentional about our lives if we are ever going to bring balance and level up. From relationships to hobbies, we can't ever let one take center stage and dominate the rest. We must give appropriate focus to each, depending on the season of life we're in. I use Mark 8:36 as a reminder of the importance of focus: "And what do you benefit if you gain the whole world but lose your own soul?" What good is it to have a bunch of money or material possessions if we lose our lives, our spouses, or our peace because we are out of balance? This is why we must bring intentional balance to our lives.

Rest. We have got to learn to rest, to recharge, and to relax. We need regular Sabbaths, moments of intentional rest, if we're ever going to be the best that God has called us to be. We have to rest our minds, recharge our emotions, and refocus our spirits so that we can level up. When we're too busy being busy and can't take regular breaks, we're too exhausted to level up.

Work. On the other hand, some people feel like their entire calling is to rest. They have forgotten that working and being active and responsible is also part of our calling. It's part of living a balanced life. Having a livelihood and an occupation is part of God's plan. The Bible says that if men don't work, they will not eat (2 Thessalonians 3:10). Proverbs 16:3 says, "Commit your actions to the LORD, and your plans will succeed." Work is an important part of the balance, just as rest and living life are. But just like with everything else, there is a point when you need to clock out of work and enjoy living the rest of your life, too! It's a balancing act.

Balancing Act

Is it possible to bring balance to your life? Yes, it is. God would never ask something of us that's impossible. But balance isn't going to come by focusing on just the big things. Balance is achieved through the little, everyday choices we make.

When we rely on God to direct us, He will make sure that the Holy Spirit warns us when we're getting out of balance. He will help us to catch it early on, before it becomes a major life issue.

It won't be easy to do, of course. We can be afraid to say "no" to opportunities. We can be afraid of not living up to the expectations of this generation. We can be afraid to disappoint. But when we live in fear of what others think, we aren't prioritizing what God thinks and what He wants for us, which is so much more important if we want balance in our lives.

It's time to get our minds off of what other people say and put our focus on Jesus. It's time to live with more passion for what the Bible says. Sure, we will get distracted at times. We'll have to push pause on the game of life and recalibrate every now and then. But as long as our power source is plugged into our Savior, we'll have what we need to balance things out and keep going.

When we live in this kind of harmony, we'll level up. We'll experience every aspect of life more closely to the way God originally intended, and we'll stay the course He set for us.

Who is God calling you to be? What balance do you need to achieve? Live intentionally with this mindset and watch as you level up to a blessed life.

Chapter Eight
G.P.S. Exercises

G (Growth): Would you describe your life as balanced and intentional or rushed and chaotic? For you, what does the next level look like? What personal or spiritual growth do you long to see in your life? Write out this goal for leveling up.

_____

_____

_____

_____

_____

_____

_____

_____

_____

_____

_____

_____

_____

_____

_____

_____

_____

_____

P (Process): Where is your life out of balance? Examine the ways you use your time, money, and physical strength. Are you being purposeful about prioritizing the things that you say are most important to you, e.g. family relationships or church involvement? Is your relationship with Jesus truly the most important thing in your life? What evidence bears this out? What are the top two or three things you need to change to see your life become balanced?

_____

_____

_____

_____

_____

_____

_____

_____

_____

_____

_____

_____

_____

_____

_____

_____

_____

_____

_____

_____

S (System): Memorize Proverbs 3:5–6 and begin to implement each portion of it in your life and decision-making. Are you committed to trusting God and following Him, even when it doesn't make sense from a human perspective? In what areas are you depending on your own understanding rather than

seeking God's will? Begin praying about every decision and commitment of your time and resources.
What can you free up from your life so that you have
time, energy, and focus to work on your goals for
leveling up?

_____

_____

_____

_____

_____

_____

_____

_____

_____

_____

_____

_____

_____

_____

_____

_____

_____

_____

Chapter Eight Notes

CHAPTER NINE

Fuel Up:
Spiritually Upgrading Your Life

If you're a frequent flyer, have you ever found yourself longing to be upgraded from economy to first class? Just imagine the extra leg room, the added comfort, the amenities and larger menu. All of these things make first class a desirable upgrade from coach. They make it a better flying experience.

God has an upgraded experience for you spiritually, too. He offers a better experience in our relationships, in our understanding of Him, in our prayer lives, in our giving, in our thinking, and in our attitude. These upgrades are available to us in the form of baptism and the person of the Holy Spirit, and they are essential stops on the map that God has for us.

Go and Be Baptized

Matthew 28:19 says, "Therefore, go and make disciples of all the nations, baptizing them in the name of the Father and the Son and the Holy Spirit." Baptism is a sign of a true upgrade in our walk with God!

When people are baptized, they are totally immersed in water and brought up out of it again. You go under, and you come back up. This symbolizes the death, burial, and resurrection of Jesus Christ. When Jesus died, He was buried. He was condemned to death to provide the sacrifice needed to secure our salvation. And when He rose again, when He was resurrected back to life, He came back up with our freedom in His possession. Our baptism identifies us with what Jesus did for us, showing that we have accepted Him as the Savior who changes our lives in a transformative way—the biggest, best life upgrade possible!

When you make the confession of faith and receive baptism, you are symbolically buried with Him, putting to death your old life, and then raised into the new life He gave to you when you received Him. You don't go back to the old you. You shouldn't even *miss* the old you.

When I was growing up, my nickname was Butch. I know, but it's true. That's how everyone knew me. I remember deciding one day to declare to my family, "I am no longer Butch. My name is Lee. Butch is dead. I have been baptized." I would intentionally not respond to people who called me Butch because I was no longer Butch. I was Lee. I was a new person in Christ, and I wanted my name to reflect that. Baptism doesn't mean that every area of your life is made perfect in that moment, but it does mean that He is Lord over every area of life.

Jesus recognized the importance of upgrading through baptism. In Mark 1:9–11, He was baptized by John the Baptist in the Jordan. Think about that! Jesus didn't exempt Himself from this significant act. He wanted baptism to be part of His relationship with His Father.

You may have the mindset that you don't need to be baptized. You may think that you will be fine without it. But if it was important enough for Jesus to be baptized, it's all the more important for us! We need this upgrade, so the enemy will do everything he can to sabotage it, even convince us that we don't need to do it.

If you do get baptized, the enemy will try to make you feel like you're the same person after baptism that you were before. He'll try to make you forget that you were raised up with Jesus, out of the water, and dedicated to living a new life. These are tricks of the enemy, who is a thief and a destroyer (John 10:10).

It's time that those of us who have been baptized start to see ourselves living the upgraded life, not swayed by the ebb and flow of our emotions. We must be unmoved by negative thoughts and only moved by the word of God! We need to remember that God's grace and favor are now ours; we only need to accept them. We are free to upgrade and live a new life.

Receive the Holy Spirit

We aren't on our own when it comes to living a new life after baptism. The Holy Spirit now lives in us to guide us and continue moving us toward an upgraded life.

The Spirit is like a spiritual technician. He knows how to help us stay connected to the power of God. We are helpless to improve ourselves on our own, but with the Spirit, we grow and change.

> *If you love me, obey my commandments. And I will ask the Father, and he will give you another Advocate, who will never leave you. He is the Holy Spirit, who leads into all truth. The world cannot receive him, because it isn't looking for him and doesn't recognize him. But you know him, because he lives with you now and later will be in you.*
>
> *—John 14:15–17*

As Christians, we need the power, wisdom, and guidance of the Holy Spirit in our lives to power our new, upgraded life that Jesus paid for us to have. All you have to do is say, "God, I receive You into my heart in Jesus' name. Forgive me and wash me clean. Amen." Then the Holy Spirit will come and begin to work on that upgrade you so desperately need.

Life with the Holy Spirit

I believe that when you keep your heart right toward Him, He will arrange every situation and circumstance critical for your success (Romans 8:28). You may not always hear what He is saying, but that doesn't mean He is not speaking. When you quiet yourself and tune into His voice, you will find the power, wisdom, and guidance of the Holy Spirit you need to live the upgraded life you are called to as a believer. Romans 8:14–16 explains:

> For all who are led by the Spirit of God are children of God. So you have not received a spirit that makes you fearful slaves. Instead, you received God's Spirit when he adopted you as his own children. Now we call him, "Abba, Father." For his Spirit joins with our spirit to affirm that we are God's children.

The Bible also emphasizes the importance of us being open to God's direction. In the words of Psalm 37:23, "The LORD directs the steps of the godly. He delights in every detail of their lives." The Holy Spirit is available to help us, partner with us, and guide us so that we can live the upgraded life God desires us to live.

Many times, I wanted just to give someone a piece of my mind and take things into my own hands, but then I would hear the small voice of the Holy Spirit inside. He would say quietly, "Let Me handle that." I had the choice to live the upgraded life and hand it over to Him or to continue to live like my old self and try to handle things on my own.

When you have the favor of God on you, the Lord will take care of you. Not long ago, I brought twenty dollars to church to buy some Girl Scout cookies. But when I reached into my pocket, the money was gone. I prayed for God to help the money find its way back to me, and right then, as I was praying, one of the pastors returned my twenty dollars he had just found.

The Holy Spirit helps us even in the small things. He cares about something small, like that twenty dollars I lost, just like He cares about the major things in my life. We just need to connect to Him in every single thing. We don't have to do this life on our own. We don't have to accept the economy class of the plane when, spiritually, we can have an upgraded experience.

The Bible says in John 16:13–15, "When the Spirit of truth comes, he will guide you into all truth. He will not speak on his own but will tell you what he has heard. He will tell you about the future. He will bring me glory by telling you whatever he receives from me. All that belongs to the Father is mine; this is why I said, 'The Spirit will tell you whatever he receives from me.'"

Did you know that it's the Spirit's job to assist you in times of prayer? The Bible promises that He will tell you things that will happen. He will guide your life and decision-making process. He will poke at your heart. He is a direct connection to the mind of God, and He is living inside of us believers, waiting to help us! But we must learn to hear Him, loud and clear.

Surround Sound, Loud and Clear

A few years ago, when I was taking my daughters to school, my youngest asked, "Dad, does God have a cell phone?"

I sat there and wondered how I was going to address this. "Well, no, baby, He doesn't have a cell phone."

Then she asked me, "How does He speak to you?"

It's a cute story, but when I reflect on it, I can't help but think that this very question is one every child of God should be asking: "How can I hear the voice of God, loud and clear?"

The voice of God doesn't have to be distorted or confusing. It can be clear every time. John 10:27 says, "My sheep listen to my voice; I know them, and they follow me." This verse makes it very clear that God wants an intimate and interactive relationship with those of us who have accepted Him as our Lord and Savior.

He is speaking even now. God is always speaking, but we allow other voices to come in and become distractions that hinder us from hearing God's voice concerning our lives and situations. We let those other voices become louder in our hearts and minds than God's voice.

Often we miss the voice of God in our lives because we're focused on feelings, traditions, other people's opinions, and so many other things that simply don't matter as much as He matters. We think that they're important and worth our time, but they're not! Isaiah 55:8–9 says, "'My thoughts are nothing like your thoughts,' says the LORD. 'And my ways are far beyond anything you could imagine. For just as the heavens are higher than the earth, so my ways are higher than your ways and my thoughts higher than your thoughts.'"

The enemy compounds this problem. He tries everything he can to keep us from hearing God's voice. He comes up against us with plans and strategies to muffle God's voice in our lives. And what he uses against one person may not be what he uses against another.

How do we fight against this? What tools do we have that we can use to drown out the other voices, as well as the voice of our enemy?

Speak, Lord

Matthew 4:1–11 tells of when Jesus was tempted. The enemy took Jesus into the wilderness and tempted Him three times. Each time, Jesus responded with scripture. He went straight to the source of truth and used *that* to overcome the enemy's temptations.

While our hobbies, interests, goals, and relationships change, the Bible does not. We must decide with our whole hearts that the word of God will be the source we turn to when it comes to hearing the voice of God. This—the scriptures of the Bible—is one tool we can use and trust.

God places a high priority on us hearing His voice, but we have to get ourselves in a position to hear Him clearly. We can't expect Him to do all His talking while we're at church! We can't expect Him to scream at us to get our attention, either. Rather, we need to put ourselves in a position to hear from Him every day.

In addition to that, we also have to wait for Him to speak. We wait for so many things in life. We wait for things to go on sale, for a job opportunity, for our turn to ride a roller coaster, for our favorite meal to be cooked at a restaurant. We wait for our teams to make it to the playoffs. So why is it so hard to wait on God? Why are we so impatient with Him?

Habakkuk 2:1–3 says, "I will climb up to my watchtower and stand at my guardpost. There I will wait to see what the LORD says and how he will answer my complaint. Then the LORD said to me, 'Write my answer plainly on tablets, so that a runner can carry the correct message to others. This vision is for a future time. It describes the end, and it will be fulfilled. If it seems slow in coming, wait patiently, for it will surely take place. It will not be delayed.'"

How did Habakkuk end up with this kind of attitude?

- He knew that the voice of God is personal. God has a word for you (Psalm 34:4, 6).

- He knew that the voice of God is powerful; it will override the circumstances (Psalm 29:4).

- He knew that the voice of God is peaceful. It brings comfort in the midst of the storm (Isaiah 54:10).

- He knew that the voice of God is purposeful; He does not speak just to speak (Joshua 21:45).

- He knew that the voice of God is persistent. He "is the same yesterday, today, and forever" (Hebrews 13:8).

Habakkuk was willing to wait because he knew that the reward of hearing God's voice was worth it, and he was prepared to listen.

We Only Have to Listen

Listening to the Holy Spirit is more than just listening to your conscience. It's listening to God. Will you search the Bible, get in a quiet place, and wait to hear from Him? Do this, and He will speak loudly and clearly and tell you marvelous things you need to know!

The Bible says in Colossians 3:15, "And let the

peace that comes from Christ rule in your hearts. For as members of one body you are called to live in peace. And always be thankful."

When we listen to the Holy Spirit, we are listening for a peace that will supernaturally referee every situation. Whether we need to go or to stop, to follow our hearts or our heads, the Spirit will give us the guidance we need to make decisions. And just like there is no arguing with a baseball umpire, there is no arguing with the Holy Spirit. He is calling a fair game. He knows if something is foul. He knows when to stay away from a person or a situation, and He will call it as He sees it. But you have to be listening!

We can position ourselves to hear Him clearly when we're more focused on what the Bible says than on anything else in our lives. Spend time praying with the Holy Spirit. When you're tempted to complain or worry, go to the Holy Spirit. It's His job to help you!

Deep Communion

God's goal is not just for us to hear Him; His heart is for us to *know* Him. How do you get to know someone? You talk. You spend time together. You become open and vulnerable. You share what's inside of you with the other person.

The more time you spend with God and the more you read about Him, the clearer His voice will become. As you grow in your relationship with Him, His voice will become louder, more defined, and easier to recognize. You'll be able to pick it out amongst all the other voices shouting for your attention. This is the very type of intimate relationship He longs to have with us. Do you long to have this relationship with Him?

One way to know if your focus and primary desire in life is to make God the center of your world is what you do when life throws you a curveball, a devastation, or a disappointment. How do you handle it? Do you walk away from God, or do you run to Him?

When you have challenges in your life, do you bring God into the situation? Do those challenges cause you to say, "God, I will follow You, no matter what," or do you turn away from Him when it gets hard?

I was once speaking at a conference in Colorado Springs, Colorado, when God asked me to do something really hard, something that I initially did not want to do. I was standing there with less than a hundred dollars to my name. I had to be there for about four days, and I didn't know how I was going to make it work financially. I had to pay for all of my meals and any extra needs that would pop up.

Then the offering container came my way. I remember standing there with the workshop speakers at the conference, and I heard the voice of God speaking to me, loud and clear. He said, "I want you to give everything in your pocket."

I reached into my pocket and held on tightly to the money. I wanted to say, "Satan, you are a liar. I have to eat." I did not want to give that money away. It was all I had. I knew that giving it away could make life very hard for me. But the more I held on to it, the more clearly I heard the voice of God saying, "Give it all."

Finally, I obeyed. I knew that I had to follow God's instructions, no matter what. So, I took the money, put it in an envelope, and dropped it into the container. As I walked back to my seat, something came over me. I began worshiping God in tongues. I had no money, yet I felt so rich. My obedience to His voice made me feel so rich.

Then the head of the conference said, "I was standing there, and the Lord spoke to me about the offering that we are receiving. The Lord told me to give ten percent of it back into Lee Wilson's life."

You can imagine how overwhelmed I was! I obeyed, and God provided. I listened to God's voice, and He came through in a big way. The Spirit spoke to me loudly and clearly that day, and I responded. And God blessed me!

The Holy Spirit is a guide who can see what we cannot. He is the voice of God, ready to talk to us and help us, but He must be invited. When the Holy Spirit lives inside of us, if we allow Him to, He will lead us and make the voice of God very clear, but this can only happen after we have become Christians and, ultimately, new creations.

The Highest Upgrade

*This means that anyone who belongs to Christ has be-
come a new person. The old life is gone; a new life has
begun!*
—2 Corinthians 5:17

This verse is important because it stresses that all
things must become new if we belong to Christ. If
we're holding on to our old mindset and calling that
the voice of God, then we have a problem. The mind
of who we used to be is tainted and dangerous. It
holds lies, traditions, and worldly influences we have
to choose to release daily. The human thought life is
not the voice of God. It can't be trusted.

Titus 1:15 says, "Everything is pure to those
whose hearts are pure. But nothing is pure to those
who are corrupt and unbelieving, because their
minds and consciences are corrupted."

Remember that when we become Christians, the
Holy Spirit makes us new. He dwells in us and wakes
us up spiritually. He gives the red light of conviction
to change our ways. He gives the yellow light of caution to wait on Him. He gives the green light of peace
to move forward. And all of this comes only from an
intimate relationship with the Holy Spirit.

There is help in the upgraded life. There is peace.
There is guidance. It starts with baptism and ends
with the Holy Spirit living in you and directing your
path along God's map, each and every step of the
way.

Chapter Nine G.P.S. Exercises

G (Growth): Do you live life on your own, or do you listen to and follow the leading of the Holy Spirit in both large and small matters? How would you like to see the Holy Spirit work in your life? Write out your goal for growth in understanding His role and relationship in your life.

_____

_____

_____

_____

_____

_____

_____

_____

_____

_____

_____

_____

_____

_____

_____

_____

_____

_____

_____

_____

_____

P (Process): What other voices are loud in your life? What makes it hard for you to hear God's voice? How can you hush these other voices and keep your focus on hearing the Holy Spirit? How can being obedient to being baptized and living from the Bible aid you in discerning God's voice?

_____

_____

_____

_____

_____

_____

_____

_____

_____

_____

_____

_____

_____

_____

_____

_____

_____

_____

_____

_____

_____

_____

_____

S (System): Set aside a specific time each day to listen to God. (This fits in naturally during your time of reading the Bible.) Be still and wait. Listen for the Holy Spirit to speak to you. Focus on growing in your relationship with Him rather than achieving a goal.

Chapter Nine Notes

_____

_____

_____

_____

_____

_____

_____

_____

_____

_____

_____

_____

_____

_____

_____

_____

_____

_____

_____

_____

_____

_____

_____

_____

CHAPTER TEN

You Have Arrived: The Pursuit of Happiness

Prescription medication commercials present a picture-perfect life, don't they? Couples walk on the beach, smiling. Everyone gets a good night's rest, and life is theirs for the taking. But then the list of side effects hits, and what was an envious, beautiful life is suddenly revealed to be full of potential harm. Some medications even say that there is the possibility of death if you take the pill they're selling!

We all want the perfect, beautiful life. We want to be the couple walking on the beach. And many times, we find that we're willing to give up everything, even our own well-being, to achieve that.

Many people are living for happiness based on temporary satisfaction. That's why people jump from one job to the next, from one city to the next, from one relationship to the next, from one pill to the next. It's a search for happiness that's unending because these things don't last. They don't bring real happiness.

At some point, we have all bought into the world's idea of happiness, but earthly things don't bring the type of happiness that the Bible claims we can have. First John 2:15–17 says, "Do not love this world nor the things it offers you, for when you love the world, you do not have the love of the Father in you. For the world offers only a craving for physical pleasure, a craving for everything we see, and pride in our achievements and possessions. These are not from the Father, but are from this world. And this world is fading away, along with everything that people crave. But anyone who does what pleases God will live forever."

God didn't say that we couldn't have things. Wouldn't He want us to enjoy the things that He gives us? Yes. But He did say that we couldn't love them more than Him. He knows the deep danger in having idols.

When we hear the word *idol*, we think of people bowing down and making sacrifices to gilded or stone statues. We assume that since we aren't doing that, we're good. But an idol is *anything* in your life that is more important to you than God, whether it is a car, money, a job, a relationship—*anything*. This is why chasing after temporary, momentary pleasures is so dangerous. God says, "Listen, I don't mind you having those things, but make sure that those things don't have you!"

A few years ago, I got a brand-new truck. We had

worked our budget and sacrificed in a few places, and it all paid off when I drove the vehicle off the lot. I was so excited.

You won't believe what happened. God told me to give it to someone else! *What?!* I couldn't believe it. How could God ask me to give up the blessing He had just given me? Didn't He realize that I had been waiting and waiting to arrive at the point where I had the money to buy that truck? I had been dreaming of how it would be to drive it and how I would look riding it. That truck meant so much to me! Then I realized that maybe that was the problem.

I talked to my wife about it, and she agreed that I should be obedient, so I gave the truck to someone God had placed on my heart. It was such a difficult thing to do, but then I realized something. I was happy. My happiness wasn't wrapped up in that truck. My happiness was rooted in God. I didn't need that truck to complete my life. My obedience to my Lord and Savior made me happier than driving in that truck ever could.

The truck itself wasn't a problem. How I handled the truck and how I responded to God was the true test. So often we hold tightly to the things of this world, thinking that they will make us happy. And all the while, God is asking us to let go. He wants to show us that true happiness can only come from Him, not from all our anxious efforts to plan for the good life.

Don't Worry; Be Happy

"Don't Worry, Be Happy" is a great song,[20] but true happiness runs much deeper than that. For many people, their state of happiness is dependent on their circumstances and what is (or isn't) happening in their lives. If your plans are not happening or turning out the way you thought they should, then you are not happy. It's as simple as that. However, these misconceptions about happiness are the first thing we need to correct.

We think that to be happy, we must have what other people have. We live our lives trying to keep up with what we see on social media—bigger houses, newer cars, more elaborate vacations. Sometimes we think that we need to have more, more, more to be happy. For many of us, this is our mentality.

We also think that to be happy, we must be liked by everyone. We get stressed out over what other people say and think of us. We worry about rubbing people the wrong way, and we try to conform to what we think they want. But happiness can't come from money or things or popularity. So, what will it take?

Luke 15:11–32 tells the story of the prodigal son. It's a great example of how most of us are happy when good things are happening, but when those good things fade away, the happiness goes with them. The son in the story left his father and lived a life of pleasure, exactly as he wanted. But when the money ran out, he panicked.

The prodigal son's pursuit of happiness became his undoing. What he thought would bring happiness—money, possessions, an active social life—did so only until the moment when the money ran out. The moment he could no longer support his frivolous lifestyle was the moment his life crumbled. His happiness was built on a faulty foundation, one that couldn't support his life.

On top of this, his motives were wrong. He thought that true happiness could be found by being out on his own, doing his own thing. He thought, "As soon as I get my own place, I'll be happy." What he failed to realize was that his own place meant that he had to have his own money. What he thought would bring him more happiness in reality meant more work. He was too naïve to realize the truth. True happiness is not found in comfort or conformity, but in something far more eternal and solid, something beyond temporary happiness.

> I said to myself, "Come on, let's try pleasure. Let's look for the 'good things' in life." But I found that this, too, was meaningless.
> —Ecclesiastes 2:1

Have you ever tested things out to see if they would make you happy? Do you remember the first time you smoked or drank? You probably did so because of peer pressure, and then you kept doing it because it made you happy. You thought, "I've finally found something that makes my life easier!"

King Solomon could relate to this. Ecclesiastes 2:11 says, "But as I looked at everything I had worked so hard to accomplish, it was all so meaningless—like chasing the wind. There was nothing really worthwhile anywhere." Here was one of the wisest and wealthiest men ever to live, and he realized something: you can't buy happiness.

The secret to a happy, satisfying life is not something we can purchase at the store. True happiness is not determined by what's happening around us, but by what's happening in us. True happiness is only found in a personal relationship with God.

Joy in My Heart

Listen, I get it. Life is rough. Sometimes it's hard to focus on our relationship with God. It's hard to find that joy when so much is falling apart around us, but I promise you that your circumstances are temporary. What's *happening to you* is a season of life, like spring following winter. But what is *happening in you*, that is your responsibility all the time, no matter the season of life.

I used to work for Sears in the auto department, putting tires on cars. One day, I was taking some tires off a Suburban and wasn't paying attention. I got my hand stuck between the tire and the rim—a very dangerous situation.

In that moment, I had to make a choice. I could

let my circumstances affect my entire outlook on life, or I could hold tightly to the God I knew loved and cared for me and who gave me all my joy and contentment.

Don't get me wrong—I was concerned. The first thing that came to my mind was that my hand was never going to be the same again. When they cut the tire to free my hand, it was completely flat. Lifeless.

I started confessing the scriptures from the Bible, believing that God had a plan in this and that He would get me through, no matter the outcome. A friend took me to the hospital, praying in the Holy Spirit the entire time. I couldn't look at my hand. I refused to be caught up in the emotion of the moment and moved by what I saw. I made the choice to be happy and thank the Lord, no matter what I felt and no matter what my hand looked like.

At the hospital, I asked the staff to refrain from saying anything negative. All I wanted was an X-ray and a straightforward prognosis. I didn't need any of the worry, fear, or anxiety that often comes with situations like this one.

I remember that my hand was hurting and pounding, but I refused to let it shake my faith. I refused to let what anyone said move me. I refused to let the entire circumstance change my heart toward God. He was Lord, no matter what!

The X-rays came out, and the doctors were in disbelief. My hand was fine—no nerve or muscle damage, no broken bones. I would make a complete recovery. They wrote me a prescription for pain medication, and that was it!

In that situation, the enemy wanted me to move to a position of panic and fear. He wanted me to take my trust away from God. He wanted to steal my joy. If he had done that, I'm convinced that the enemy would have taken my happiness. He would have proven that when things get serious, I *don't* trust in God!

Thankfully, that wasn't the case. But how many times in life do we allow the enemy to succeed in doing just that? How many times does he take a situation and cause us to lose sight of the hope we have in God? How often do we tell God, "I'm going to take my trust back from You. I'm going to take my faith back, too, because this situation is just too much for me to handle"?

When we do this, our relationship with God suffers. We experience setbacks because we allow our joy and happiness to be rooted in the unstable things of this world rather than in the only one who is truly unshakable, God.

Happiness in Him

So many of us are striving to find happiness. We think that we can find it in people, places, and things. We think that if we just have more money, more friends, more popularity, then we'll be happy.

But the reality is that true happiness is found in following God and taking the path He has for us.

Taking the path of fulfillment and happiness in God doesn't come without struggle. At every turn, the enemy will attack. He'll do his best to take our focus from God and to show that when life gets hard, we *don't* fully believe His promises.

That's why we have to stay strong. Yes, life is hard! Yes, bad things can happen! But whom do we trust, the maker of the universe or ourselves? When we rest in Him, believing that He will see us through, no matter the outcome, then we will find true happiness, true contentment, and true faith for the incredible journey He has for us.

Chapter Ten G.P.S. Exercises

G (Growth): Where do you look for your happiness? Write out your personal definition of happiness and your goal for a happy heart and life.

_____

_____

_____

_____

_____

_____

_____

_____

_____

_____

_____

_____

_____

_____

_____

_____

_____

_____

_____

_____

_____

P (Process): What circumstances are stealing your joy and tempting you to doubt God and His goodness? How can you view these same circumstances with faith? How can you worship and trust God in the midst of these difficulties?

_____

_____

_____

_____

_____

_____

_____

_____

_____

_____

_____

_____

_____

_____

_____

_____

_____

_____

_____

_____

S (System): Commit now to seeking your happiness by following God and pursuing a relationship with Him instead of trying to find happiness from your circumstances or possessions. Select a few go-to worship songs and/or Bible passages that you can turn to when life starts to get hard.

_____

_____

_____

Chapter Ten Notes

CONCLUSION

Map Your Life: Fulfill Your Purpose!

Yes, my friend, you have a purpose. You are destined for an incredible journey. The only question is: Are you navigating this life in a way that allows you to fulfill that purpose? Will you be part of a generation that chooses to live on purpose for God?

Now you have the tools you need. You know the importance of getting into the word of God every single day. You know the power of prayer and time alone with God. You know that you need to guard the words of your mouth and take care of your thought life. You know how to get rid of toxic relationships and trust God to show up in big ways.

You know to ask for His guidance and help. You know to be baptized and to listen to the Holy Spirit. You know that time is short. God has something for you *now*! There is no room and no time for hesitation! You know these things because you have this map.

If you haven't yet begun your journey toward getting unstuck and entering into the abundant, purposeful life that God has for you, I challenge you to give it a try. Give God *thirty days* to make a difference in your heart. Seek Him, pray to Him, and read His word. I promise that He will show up. He will reveal to you where you are stuck, even in places you didn't realize you were stuck! What's even better is that He won't leave you stuck. He will offer you a way through. He will show you how to navigate your way toward His purpose for your life. He will take you from *here* to *there*.

It's time to live the life that you were meant to live. It's time to map your life in the direction God has set for you, the only route that will bring you real happiness and fulfillment. It's time to live your life on purpose.

WORKBOOK

Conclusion G.P.S. Exercises

G (Growth): Think back over all you have learned in this book and review the goals that you set for each chapter. What is your big take away, the area where God is really speaking to you about changes you need to make? Write out your thirty-day goal for growth in your relationship with God and finding His purpose for you.

_____

_____

_____

_____

_____

_____

_____

_____

_____

_____

_____

_____

_____

_____

_____

_____

_____

_____

_____

_____

_____

_____

_____

P (Process): What things do you need to stop doing and what things do you need to start doing in order to fulfill your goal? Where are you stuck? After reading this book, what is your map to becoming unstuck?

_____

_____

_____

_____

_____

_____

_____

_____

_____

_____

_____

_____

_____

_____

_____

_____

_____

_____

_____

_____

_____

_____

_____

S (System): What new habits and accountability are you putting into place in your life in order to stay faithful in the changes you have made and in growing in your relationship with God?

Conclusion Notes

_____

_____

_____

_____

_____

_____

_____

_____

_____

_____

_____

_____

_____

_____

_____

_____

_____

_____

_____

_____

REFERENCES

Notes

1. *New Oxford American Dictionary*, "procrastination." 3rd ed. In Dictionary (app). Apple, Inc.

2. Lexico, "procrastinate." https://www.lexico.com/en/definition/procrastinate.

3. "National Procrastination Week." National Day Calendar. https://nationaldaycalendar.com/national-procrastination-week-first-two-weeks-in-march-or-when-its-convenient/.

4. Korkki, Phyliss. "Driven to Worry, and to Procrastinate." *New York Times.* February 5, 2012. https://www.nytimes.com/2012/02/26/jobs/procrastinating-at-work-maybe-youre-overwhelmed.html.

5. Kelley, Michael B. "Expert: Michael Jackson Was the Only Person Ever to Go 60 Days Without 'Real Sleep.'" Business Insider. June 21, 2013.

https://www.businessinsider.com/michael-jackson-didnt-sleep-2013-6 July 21, 2013.

6. *Liber Facetiarum: Being a Collection of Curious and Interesting Anecdotes.* D. Akenhead and Sons, 1809, p. 182. In Hathi Trust Digital Library. https://babel.hathitrust.org/cgi/pt?id=nyp.33433074922000&view=1up&seq=204.

7. Luther King, Martin. "Beyond Vietnam." April 4, 1967. Transcript of audio speech. The Martin Luther King, Jr. Research and Education Institute, Stanford University. https://kinginstitute.stanford.edu/king-papers/documents/beyond-vietnam.

8. Juarez, Ilian. "Mary Pipher's 'I Am From' in Art Application & Poetic Expression for Identity Exploration." *Multicultural Education* 25, no. 1, Caddo Gap Press, October 2017, p. 48.

9. *New Oxford American Dictionary*, "detox." 3rd ed. In Dictionary (app). Apple, Inc.

10. Blue Letter Bible, "Strong's H5341 – *natsar.*" https://www.blueletterbible.org/lang/lexicon/lexicon.cfm?Strongs=H5341&t=NLT.

11. Blue Letter Bible, "Lexicon: Strong's H4929 – *mishmar.*" https://www.blueletterbible.org/lang/lexicon/lexicon.cfm?Strongs=H4929&t=NLT.

12. Arlington National Cemetery. "The Tomb of the Unknown Soldier." https://www.arlingtoncemetery.mil/

Explore/Tomb-of-the-Unknown-Soldier.

13. American Historama. "Tomb of the Unknown Soldier Guards." http://www.american-historama.org/1913-1928 -ww1-prohibition-era/tomb-of-the-unknown-soldier- guards.htm.

14. *New Oxford American Dictionary*, "renew." 3rd edition. In Dictionary (app). Apple, Inc.

15. Brandreth, Gyles. *How to Have Fun with 860,341,500 Words*. William Morrow & Co., 1980.

16. Bardi, Jason. "Secrets of Human Speech Uncovered: Work at UCSF Shows Brain Experts Symphony-Like Control of Vocal Tract During the Act of Speaking." University of California San Francisco. 2013. https://www.ucsf.edu/news/2013/02/104531/secrets- human-speech-uncovered.

17. *New Oxford American Dictionary*, "toxic." 3rd edition. In Dictionary (app). Apple, Inc.

18. *New Oxford American Dictionary*, "love." 3rd edition. In Dictionary (app). Apple, Inc.

19. *New Oxford American Dictionary*, "hate." 3rd edition. In Dictionary (app). Apple, Inc.

20. McFerrin, Bobby. "Don't Worry, Be Happy." Track 1, *Don't Worry-Be Happy!* EMI-Manhattan Records, 1988. https://www.discogs.com/Bobby-McFerrin-Dont-Worry- Be-Happy/release/743558.

About the Author

After growing up the oldest of five siblings in the projects of Houston, Texas, Lee Wilson made it his mission to teach and reach people around the globe. With over thirty years of ministry experience, Lee has spoken in over 200 cities in America, as well as Africa, the Dominican Republic, Russia, Japan, Australia, Honduras, Canada, and Mexico. Wherever he finds himself, his primary goal is to help others define their God-given purpose and instill in them the belief that there is no substitute for a life filled with purpose that extends well beyond its end. Lee cares greatly for young people, and lets this passion drive him in his positions as a Lead Pastor, Youth Pastor, Mentor, Executive Pastor, Founder of Face2Face National Youth Conference, the Creator of the Life On Purpose podcast, the NexGen Masterclass and leewilson.life. His dedication to intentional living inspired his career as an author, leadership coach, and board director for multiple non-profit organizations. Lee has inspired thousands to embrace their unique purpose, changing and challenging mindsets for the better. At the writing of this book, Lee lives in Syracuse, New York with his beautiful wife, Tonya. They have two daughters, Alexis and Jordan.